"Your core values are the deeply ingrained principles that guide all of your company's actions; they serve as its cultural cornerstones."

Howard Schultz, former CEO of Starbucks

Create a high performing business culture and unleash your business potential.

Copyright

ISBN   978-1-952359-55-2   (hardcover)
ISBN   978-1-952359-51-4   (paperback)
ISBN   978-1-952359-52-1   (ebook)

For More Information
About the Life Planning Series:

www.lifeplanningtools.com

POWERFUL
Business Strategies

Implementing Core Values
For Business Success

J. S. Wellman

J.S. WELLMAN

Extra-mile Publishing

For Individual Employees
{Employee Core Value Handbook}

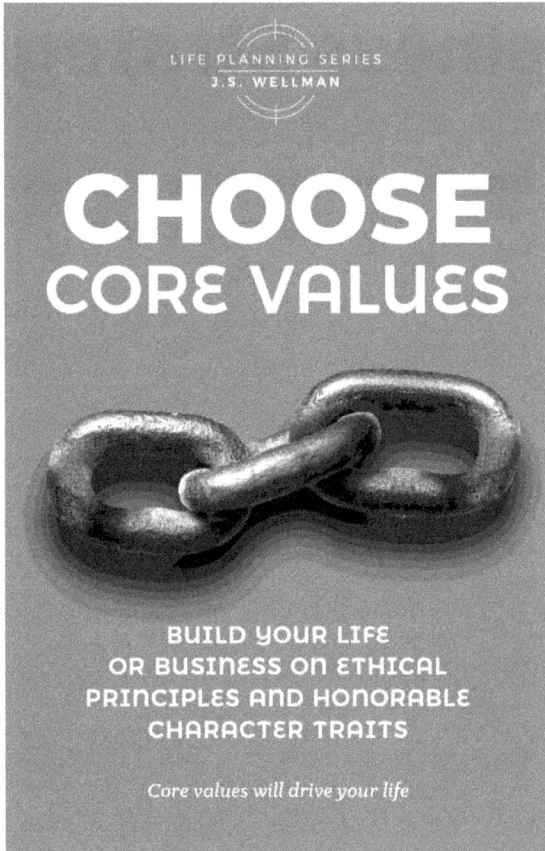

Obtain this book at:
https://www.amazon.com/dp/195235949X

Table of Contents

INTRODUCTION

"Strategy is about making choices, trade-offs;
it's about deliberately choosing to be different."
Michael Porter, Prf. Harvard Business School

WHO SHOULD READ THIS BOOK?

This book is generally intended for company owners, directors, executives, managers, and supervisors. In particular it is for the human resource department or other third-party that may be developing or leading training sessions for company employees.

The sub-title of the book describes its purpose: ***Implementing Core Values For Business Success.*** It is written for employers who want to develop, implement, or improve the core values in their business. It contains twelve business values that might be adopted by a company. In addition, there are two subjects in the Appendices (leadership and decision-making) that are very important skills needed for a successful business. Good leadership skills will be essential in implementing a business culture based on the company's core values. Some might include leadership as a core value, but we believe it is the skill necessary to successfully implement core values in a business.

No one would adopt all the twelve core values we discuss in this book. Typically an employer would have four to six core values and often one of those would be primary in the business culture or operations.

THE PURPOSE OF THIS BOOK

The purpose of this book is to describe the importance and nature of the most common business core values. In addition we provide additional practical help in each chapter to assist in the training of employees in these core values. At the end of each chapter we include:

- Practical tips for helping employees adopt the core value.
- Discussion questions to be used for large or small group meetings with employees.
- Group exercises that can be used to teach the core value.

In addition, Appendix A is an outline of how training programs can be developed and implemented using this book and the book, *"CHOOSE Core Values"* which is a separate book in our Life Planning Series for employees describing sixteen personal core values.

TRAINING APPROACH or STRATEGY

We believe that in implementing a business core value strategy it is necessary to develop that core value in the individual employees. If the desired core value is not instilled in the employees to some degree there will be little hope that an effective strategy can be implemented within the company.

You can't train someone to be "HONEST" when they are at work and on the job unless that is consistent with their normal behavior away from the workplace.

If you want INNOVATION to be a core value of your business you must train employees to be adaptable, flexible, open-minded, and curious.

Therefore, the necessary strategy is not to promote the specific core values of the company but to teach and train individuals to be the kind of people that produce that result. You want employees to personally live by the chosen standard in order to reap the benefits of their inherent belief in that core value.

If you want your company to be CUSTOMER-ORIENTED your employees need to be empathetic toward others, friendly, good communicators, and excellent at problem-solving. One might argue that in training employees to be customer-oriented you never actually talk about being "customer-oriented," because it has so little inherent meaning to an employee. A company that is customer-oriented is one that effectively meets the real need or solves the real problem of the customer. The employee can't help customers unless they know and understand customer needs and have an ability to help them find solutions to problems.

> **High performing leaders and teams are looking**
> **for ways to gain competitive advantage.**
> **High performance is often associated with**
> **the existence of core values.**

WHY IMPLEMENT CORE VALUES IN YOUR BUSINESS

Adopting core values for a business can bring numerous benefits that contribute to its success and growth. Here are ten important reasons for adopting and implementing core values in your business.

1. Decision-Making: Core values provide a clear framework for decision-making at all levels of the organization, ensuring that choices align with the company's principles and long-term goals.

2. Company Culture: Core values create a shared identity and sense of purpose among employees, fostering a cohesive and motivated workforce that works collaboratively toward common goals.

3. Employee Engagement: When employees feel connected to a set of meaningful core values, their job satisfaction and engagement increase, leading to higher productivity and lower turnover rates. They feel a real part of the business.

4. Business Ethics: Core values serve as an ethical compass, helping the business maintain integrity, transparency, and ethical conduct in its operations and interactions.

5. Customer Loyalty: Companies that live by their core values tend to build trust and credibility with customers, leading to stronger brand loyalty and true customer satisfaction.

6. Competitive Advantage: Core values can set a business apart from its competitors by highlighting its unique strengths, priorities, and commitment to certain principles.

7. Strategic Alignment: A company's core values guide the development of policies and strategies, ensuring that business initiatives and goals are aligned with its overarching values and beliefs.

8. Innovation: Core values can encourage a culture of innovation and adaptability, empowering employees to think creatively and embrace change to stay relevant in a dynamic market.

9. Leadership: Leaders who embody and promote core values provide a strong confirmation of the business values to their teams, leading to more effective and consistent leadership practices throughout the organization.

10. Reputation: A business with well-defined core values is likely to earn a positive reputation in its industry and community, attracting partners, investors, and top talent who share those values.

Incorporating core values into a business's foundation can lead to a more purpose-driven, ethical, and successful organization that positively impacts its employees, customers, suppliers, and even society at large.

> **IMPORTANT NOTE:** This book is a training guide for the employer, but it is intended to be used with another book, *CHOOSE Core Values,* that is for the individual employee. The *CHOOSE* book is in our Life Planning Series and can be obtained at: **https://www.amazon.com/dp/195235949X**

THE LIFE PLANNING SERIES

As indicated above, this book is intended to be used with *Choose Core Values*. That series is directed at <u>individuals</u> who want to improve personal character traits in order to live a better or improved life.

Each book in the Series addresses one particular subject, helping an individual identify his life goals and guiding him in creating action plans to achieve that particular goal. *CHOOSE Core Values* in that Series is <u>different.</u> Rather than one subject there are sixteen, each of which relates in some way to the corporate core values in this book.

For example, both books contain specific chapters on integrity, personal growth, honor and respect, accountability, and equality/diversity. In addition many of the other traits in the *CHOOSE* book relate to the business core values of quality, being customer-oriented, being results-oriented, innovation, teamwork, social responsibility, and fun.

The Series also addresses topics like integrity, choosing friends, guarding your speech, working with diligence, making sound financial decisions, having a positive self-image, leadership, faith, love and family, and the book on core values referred to above.

CONSEQUENCES

Businesses are constantly making choices about both significant and insignificant issues. Choices shape the course of a company's future. The actual consequences you experience will vary depending on the business circumstances, but there will be consequences nonetheless. The degree of the consequence will also vary, but you should not be fooled into thinking small actions are insignificant. Even small actions can produce significant consequences.

In a number of proverbs, King Solomon suggests that doing what is right is to be preferred over doing evil. King Solomon was known world-wide for his great wisdom and argued that it is better to be on the side of the righteous. The reasoning is the same as the man who builds his business or life on rock versus sand. If we build on sand (questionable ways) then our hopes and plans will never stand up against the storms of life or competition in business. If we build on rock (high character) our plans will hold firm.

We reap what we sow and if we sow badly, because we rejected or ignored what is right, the wise counsel of friends, or important core values, we will reap the negative consequences.

> *"The essence of strategy is*
> *choosing what not to do."*
> Michael Porter

INTENTIONALITY

We believe that an important key to success for implementing any of these core values is ***intentionality.*** You can talk and plan, but unless you actually do something, the result will be nothing. All the slick presentations, advertising, and promotions come to nothing unless someone buys the product. Just reading this book, thinking about core values, or even identifying your core values, will not improve your company unless you do something.

Progress requires some form of self-discipline or intentionality. You must be prepared, proactive, and focused. Being successful is not luck and it does not happen by accident. You must do something if you want something to happen. This is true for both the employee on the assembly line, the professional in the corner office, and the company that wants to be successful.

It generally requires that you have a plan and focus on that plan to achieve your business objectives. Core values have to be a priority if you want them to impact your business. There may be difficulties during the implementation period. Nothing important ever comes without a cost. The question will be, "How committed are you to the goal?" One major attribute of successful people, leaders, and companies is that they don't give up if things get difficult.

Whether you are an employee, executive, or owner you should take pride in work that is well done. Implementing core values in your business in order to be successful is not the same as designing attractive packaging that will catch the eye of the consumer. Core values represent who and what you are as a business. Some might describe it as your *brand*.

Henry Ford said that you cannot build a reputation on what you are *going to do*. He means we must actually do or produce something of high value. Promises only count if they are met. Marketing slogans are useful only if they are true.

Empty promises, poor quality products, or uncaring customer service will not be useful in establishing a company brand or reputation.

Quality products require excellence. Thus, the personal employee characteristics of being honest, diligent, trustworthy, and dependable are highly valued in a workplace dedicated to core values.

"Things may come to those who wait,
but only the things left by those who hustle."
Abraham Lincoln

Chapter 1
Honesty, Integrity, and Truth

*"One word of truth
outweighs the whole world."*
Alexander Solzhenitsyn

GENERAL

Honesty and *Integrity* must be the fundamental core values of any individual or company. Of the core values discussed in this book, the most fundamental are truth, honesty, and integrity which produce trust and respect. If you adhere to these values, it is much easier to achieve success. They are the gateways to almost all other core values.

Any contractor or builder will tell you that the most important part of a house is the foundation. A foundation that is not level and setting on solid ground will create problems in every phase of the building process. Problems can become so great that the construction ultimately may need to be torn out. Honesty and integrity must be the foundational core values of your organization.

If you operate with integrity, you will inherently possess a number of other good core values as an organization. Integrity will mean you are dependable and reliable, which will normally produce a good reputation. If you are truthful you will be incorruptible in your dealings with customers. You will not cheat to gain some competitive advantage. You will not be devious or deceptive in your marketing. This is why honesty, integrity, and truth are the cornerstones for an outstanding organization. It is why many businesses include some version of these characteristics in their core values.

***Make it a primary goal to be honest,
operate with integrity, and stand on truth!***

HONESTY

Honesty means that you speak the truth. You do not lie. It means that you do not cheat anybody. You would not defraud, deceive, misguide, or misinform anyone.

This concept can be illustrated by the color white. If something is true and honest, then it is pure white. If there is any gray then it is no longer white. It may be referred to as dirty white, off-white, or cream. Truth and honesty are like that. They are pure. There is no such thing as partial truth. Something is either true or it is not true.

You are either honest or you're not honest. If there is any gray mixed into your truth, then it is no longer true. Little white lies should be called little gray lies. Partial truth and partial honesty do not exist.

Honesty in all things

If you are honest, you will be honest in both big and small things. It doesn't matter if it is over-charging for shipping or selling defective products. The honest company does neither. There is no such thing as a little lie, a little deception, or a little cheating. If a company cheats at little things it most likely will cheat at big things. An honest company is honest with pennies as well as with millions.

Customers gravitate toward companies they can trust. They want honesty and dependability in all aspects of a customer-business relationship.

> *"If a person doesn't lie,*
> *he won't have that much to remember!"*
> Abe Lincoln

Don't follow the crowd

You can't do business in some countries, and even with some city or state governments, without paying bribes. Dishonesty left unchecked becomes a cancer controlling how business is conducted.

Cheating can become so bad that dishonesty becomes the norm. When the general public decides everyone is doing it, they believe they must also cheat in order to survive. This is what happened in the sport of professional bicycle racing between 1990 and 2010. You may have heard about the drug scandals involving Lance Armstrong. But Armstrong was not the only one cheating. The sport was overrun by cheating and drug abuse.

Then, of course, the cover-up begins. Everyone lies about the true environment, hoping not to be caught. The sad thing is that the lying just builds up until it explodes. The liars begin thinking that what they are doing is acceptable and not really dishonest. They actually believe their own lies. They may even have a very high opinion of themselves while they are living a lie. But eventually the lie is exposed and the inevitable cover-up begins, leading to the undeniable result that dishonesty reigns! Then the lies evaporate and the liars are exposed!

Dishonest companies will eventually be caught or found out. Fortunes can be lost and reputations destroyed. Businesses can go bankrupt. The end result is that the lying owner gets caught and their dishonesty will cause various levels of difficulty, suffering, and even time in prison. Some individuals have even committed suicide because they could not live with the shame of public disclosure.

If Lance Armstrong had admitted his cheating early on and offered to help fix the problem, his life would have been much different and his standing in the eyes of society would be much higher today.

> *"I have met men who are habitual liars.*
> *They have lied so long that they no longer*
> *can distinguish between the truth and a lie."*
> Billy Graham

INTEGRITY

Integrity is the attribute of being honest, truthful, trustworthy, and compliant to a set of standards. Some might suggest that integrity is conforming to doing the right thing, even when no one is watching. A company that has integrity will be honorable and upright in all phases of its operations. It will value truth and operate by a set of defined ethical standards. Actions, not words, demonstrate whether a company operates with integrity.

> *"Your image is what people think of you*
> *and your integrity is who you really are."*
> John Maxwell

Truth is a shield

Honesty and truth can shield a company from gossip, slander, and many other forms of evil. Integrity allows a business to work in an environment with a sense of calm and security. Companies that operate in the cloudy space between right and wrong will ultimately be exposed and the result is never pretty.

Customers respect integrity

A reputation for integrity will draw people and customers to your company and to your products. Assistance is much easier to acquire when you operate with integrity compared to a businesses that is untrustworthy. Customers will not waste their time with products produced by people or companies that demonstrate dishonesty or have only a casual acquaintance with the truth.

> *One is not given integrity. It is earned by the*
> *ongoing and continual pursuit of honesty.*

COMPROMISE

In settling disputes or negotiating contracts, compromise can be rewarded. In such situations the parties are making mutual concessions or accommodations in order to arrive at a mutually agreeable result. People make mutual concessions in order to receive the benefit of a contractual agreement.

Dale Carnegie said in his book, *How to Win Friends and Influence People,* "The highest levels of influence are reached when generosity and trustworthiness surround your behavior." If you trusted someone and they were willing to give up something that was of valuable to them, would you also be willing to be generous and give up something of value? That is what typically happens in true compromise.

However, if you compromise your standards, compromise your reputation, or compromise your word, compromise becomes a cancer on your products and services.

Difficulties, struggles, or trials should not detract from your commitment to the truth. Just because business gets difficult is not a good reason for compromising your company values or business standards. If you cannot deliver on a promise, tell the truth. Nothing is gained by lying. You may gain some time, but the lie will be found out.

> *"Compromise, while at times morally necessary*
> *or at least justifiable, is more often only the*
> *first permission for a person (or society)*
> *to begin a long downhill descent."*
> Dennis Prager

Compromise in agreements

Unions and employers negotiate and compromise regularly in order to get the best deal for their constituents. The ability to compromise in this manner is considered a proper and appropriate means to produce working relationships and agreements that both parties can endorse.

Alternatively, if we won't compromise on less important or non-critical issues or in special circumstances, we are often considered hardheaded, stubborn, or obstinate. It is important to understand your circumstances and know what is important in both personal and business situations. You could choose to extend credit to an old customer who is experiencing a temporary downturn in their business even though such grace would be outside company policies. Logic and good sense should dictate whether to adhere to rules.

> *"All compromise is based on give and take,*
> *but there can be no give and take on fundamentals.*
> *Any compromise on mere fundamentals is surrender.*
> *For it is all give and no take."*
> Mahatma Gandhi

Standing firm

Don't waste time with customers who oppose or push back against your core values. Standing firm means that you ignore the peer pressure of associates or customers when the suggested action would violate the values of your organization. One way to hold fast to your values is to have coworkers and superiors who fully support you in particularly trying circumstances.

If employees feel that it would be appropriate to compromise a particular rule, policy, or core value, they should be encouraged to get permission from someone in the organization with the authority to make that exception.

> *"If you have integrity nothing else matters.*
> *If you don't have integrity nothing else matters."*
>
> Alan K. Simpson

CONCLUSION

Some believe business is a contest and they must use any and all means to win the game. Therefore being devious or deceptive is acceptable behavior because the only goal is to come out on top. These companies are often in a very competitive market and become unconcerned how they win, as long as they win. Their attitude may be to win at all costs. They may not even think of their activities as wrong, but simply the normal playing field for their industry.

But what happens when your customer finds that you were deceptive or under-handed? You quickly lose trust! Your client or customer will never want to deal with you again. Once your attitudes and shady actions are made known, your reputation can be destroyed. Deceptive people and companies are often hated (or at least greatly disliked).

Honesty and integrity will provide an atmosphere that draws others to you and your company, not away from you or your group. If you are true, sincere, and genuine, you will attract others who value the same characteristics. Truth is a magnet for customers seeking quality and value they can trust.

If you have core values, do you religiously adhere to them? Do your customers know what your core values are? What happens if and when you break a core value? How often do you find it necessary to tell lies about your products or services? Why?

Think before you speak or act.
Your reputation is important!

Leaders are the key

The practice of lying is never related to just certain subjects, therefore, a leader that lies about sales figures will also lie about what is included in the products or what the products can do. Such people will do great damage to the business.

Personal character is an integral part of the makeup of excellent leaders. If leaders cannot be trusted and take no responsibility for their actions, the organization has little hope for success, even if such leaders have many other good leadership qualities.

Honesty, integrity, and truth must start at the top and run all through an organization. Subordinates at any level will imitate the core values of their leaders. Senior leaders, in particular, must emphasize and demonstrate these qualities and encourage them throughout their organization.

Anything that is morally corrupt or illegal will be rejected out of hand by good leaders. Employees should be encouraged to report any corrupt practices to management.

Ethical leadership comes down to each individual deciding if he or she is willing to violate their core values, regardless of whether or not a Code of Conduct exists. Good leaders build their careers on a set of core values regardless of whether their organization has a formal Code. Those values vary between leaders but will normally include most of the characteristics discussed in this chapter.

Valued leaders are always accountable for their words and actions. If a good leader makes a mistake he will be the first to openly admit it.

The focus becomes on correctly identifying the error and finding effective solutions, not on blame, shame, or censure. A leader who wants honesty and integrity from his team or company must exhibit those same characteristics himself.

> *"Leadership can be defined*
> *by one word: "honesty."*
> Earl Weaver

ILLUSTRATION: Johnson & Johnson's Tylenol Crisis (1982)

In the early 1980s, Johnson & Johnson faced a crisis that put its commitment to honesty and integrity to the ultimate test. In September 1982, seven people in the Chicago area died after consuming Extra-Strength Tylenol capsules that had been tampered with and laced with cyanide.

Upon learning about the tampering, Johnson & Johnson took immediate and unprecedented action. The company prioritized the safety of its consumers over financial considerations. Within days, it issued a nationwide recall of 31 million bottles of Tylenol, worth over $100 million. The decision was made despite the absence of conclusive evidence linking the tampering to the company itself. This transparent response set a new standard for crisis management.

Johnson & Johnson worked closely with law enforcement agencies, the FBI, and the Food and Drug Administration (FDA) throughout the investigation. The company shared all information with the authorities and the public, fostering trust and demonstrating a commitment to uncovering the truth behind the tampering.

To prevent a similar incident in the future, Johnson & Johnson introduced new, tamper-evident packaging for over-the-counter medications. The company invested heavily in research and development to create triple-sealed, tamper-resistant packaging, similar to the technology widely used today.

In the aftermath of the crisis, Johnson & Johnson's actions spoke louder than words. The company's commitment to honesty, integrity, and consumer safety became a defining aspect of its corporate culture. The decisive and ethical response not only saved lives but also helped rebuild public trust in the Tylenol brand and Johnson & Johnson as a corporate citizen.

Despite the immediate financial losses, Johnson & Johnson's commitment to honesty and integrity had long-term positive effects. Johnson & Johnson's stock rebounded, and the company continued to be a leader in the pharmaceutical and consumer healthcare industries.

Conclusion: This crisis showcased how the corporate core value of honesty and integrity was a guiding force in the face of adversity. Johnson & Johnson's commitment to transparency, accountability, and consumer safety not only saved lives but also contributed to the company's reputation for ethical business practices and corporate responsibility. The case remains a powerful example of how honesty and integrity can be integral to long-term business success.[A]

PRACTICAL TIPS

- Employees should know the company values and be encouraged to stand firm when under pressure to cut corners or avoid the truth.

- Employees should be humble in dealing with customers who want to compromise company standards. A "superior" attitude is never the best attitude in a discussion with a customer about ethics or core values.

- Clients should be made aware of the company values and standards and the reasons such standards exist.

- All employees should be cautious about what they say on social media, particularly if it can be associated with the company.

- Promises to customers should be very clear and concise so there is no confusion or misunderstanding.

- Commitments to customers or suppliers should not be made if they cannot be kept.

- Employees should be encouraged to be accountable and to admit mistakes immediately.

GROUP DISCUSSION QUESTIONS

1. How do honesty, integrity, and truth contribute to building a positive company culture?

2. How do you think our company's reputation would be affected if there were a lack of honesty among employees?

3. What would happen if customers failed to trust our products or services?

4. There is an anonymous saying about compromise: "Many things are worse than defeat, and compromising with evil is one of them." Do you agree with this? Why? Why not?

5. When is compromise appropriate? Explain.

6. Why do liars need excellent memories?

7. What reasons would you list for the importance of integrity?

8. Can you give an example of honesty or integrity in our company and how it impacted employees or customers? How did it contribute to company success?

9. Are there areas in the company marketing plans or practices that push the envelope in regard to honesty and trust?

10. How can we ensure that our employees feel comfortable speaking up and sharing the truth, even when it might be difficult or unpopular?

11. Can you think of any potential challenges or obstacles that might arise when trying to establish and maintain a culture of honesty, integrity, and truth? How can we overcome them?

12. Do you think personal integrity are important in the workplace or is only the integrity of the company important?

EXERCISES

#1. Case Studies

Provide the group with a series of real or hypothetical workplace scenarios that involve ethical dilemmas. Divide the employees into smaller groups and ask them to discuss and analyze each case study, considering the principles of honesty, integrity, truth, and trust. Encourage them to share their thoughts, debate the possible solutions, and collectively decide on the most ethical course of action. After a given time period each group should present their solution to the entire group. The group with the best solution could receive a reward.

#2. Trust-building Circles

Form a circle with the employees and ask each person to share a personal experience where they had to demonstrate honesty, integrity, or truthfulness in a challenging situation. Encourage open and honest sharing. After each person shares, have the group provide feedback, support, and recognition for the values demonstrated. This exercise helps create a safe and trusting environment among employees while highlighting the importance of these qualities.

#3. Integrity in Action

Assign small groups of employees the task of creating short skits or role-plays that depict scenarios where honesty, integrity, truth, or trust are either upheld or compromised in the workplace. After each performance, engage the entire group in a discussion about the skit, focusing on the impact of the demonstrated behaviors on individuals, teams, and the overall organization.

Remember to debrief and facilitate discussions after each exercise to ensure employees understand the lessons learned and can apply them to their work environment effectively.

"Moral authority comes from following universal and timeless principles like honesty, integrity, and treating people with respect."
Stephen Covey

Chapter 2
QUALITY and EXCELLENCE

"All roads that lead to success
have to pass through
hard work boulevard at some point."
Eric Thomas

EMPLOYER: Quality and Excellence

Excellence and quality products or services can contribute, if not determine, the success and growth of an organization. A focus or core value of quality and excellence means the employer sets high standards throughout the organization for its products. Such a company will emphasize the importance of delivering products of exceptional quality. The goal is often to exceed the customer's expectations. This is more than just delivering good products to the marketplace. The objective is the pursuit of excellence in all parts of the organization.

Nothing is left to chance if the reputation and focus of an organization is quality and excellence. Employees will be trained to pay attention to detail and have a meticulous approach to their work. Employees will be encouraged to practice a work ethic that ensures tasks are executed accurately, minimizing errors, and ideally producing products with no defects.

Quality and excellence should be closely tied to meeting the real customer needs and providing exceptional product experiences. Thus, the culture and focus of customer-oriented companies is directed toward encouraging employees to understand customer requirements. The goal is to consistently deliver products that satisfy and exceed customer expectations.

Internal accountability becomes an important requirement for producing quality products and services. Employees who take ownership of their work deliver on their commitments and take responsibility for the quality of their work. Such employees are typically proactive in resolving problems or issues promptly.

Employees who value excellence in their products and services will establish quality assurance checks to ensure adherence to quality standards. This may involve implementing quality control measures or conducting regular audits.

Employers who demand quality will expect it in the ethical and professional attitudes of both their employees and suppliers. Thus, requiring integrity, transparency, and ethical decision-making is the norm. The goal is to ensure that quality is not compromised by shortcuts or unethical behavior.

Quality as an employer core value requires prioritizing continuing product improvement, customer satisfaction, attention to detail, and employee development. By promoting these characteristics and aspects within the organization, companies can enhance the overall performance of their business, build a strong brand, and drive long-term success.

> *"A dream doesn't become reality through magic;*
> *it takes sweat, determination and hard work."*
> Colin Powell

EMPLOYEE: Hard Work and Diligence

From an employee perspective the necessary character traits to produce quality products or services are hard work, working with diligence, and a desire to do their best. Such work habits will produce high quality results. The concept of being a hard worker is not only just the practice of putting out a good effort, but producing a good result.

There are several valuable benefits from an employees' perspective to working hard:

- Employees earn the respect of others. They are held in high regard for their efforts and the quality of their work.

- Such employees gain a reputation for a good work ethic and producing good results.

- The result is that they are often given special projects and are at the top end of the pay grade.

> *"The first qualification for success in my view*
> *is a strong work ethic."*
> Henry Ford II

Hard work

The advice columnist Ann Landers said, "Nobody ever drowned in his own sweat." In other words, hard work is not going to kill anyone. There are very few characteristics that are more important to an employer than finding employees who pursue excellence through diligence and hard work.

Unfortunately, some very negative attitudes and habits have developed in the workplace. There are several very common negative attitudes about work:

> 1. *Who cares? I'm bored.* Many workers are bored with their responsibilities, bored with the people they work with, and bored with life. They are bored, they are boring, and others resent their boredom. Nobody wants to work with these people and employers have no reason to keep them long.

> 2. *Questionable ethics!* Actions reveal what employees value. Issues of morality, ethics, and integrity confront employers in every line of work. Employees can cheat the employer out of time, effort, or money while on the job.

Steve Jobs took another view of work. He demanded excellence. If you have ever worked in this type of situation, you know the environment and approach to work is different. There is nothing wrong with having fun and taking breaks, but the purpose for breaks is rejuvenation, not pleasure. The workplace atmosphere is geared to challenging everyone to do their very best, to find solutions to problems that benefit the whole, not just self. Achievement is the goal.

Characteristics of diligent employees

The diligent employee who seeks excellence in his work often has many other good qualities which are beneficial to the goals of the employer. Employers want dedicated and hard-working people they can trust. Such employees generally have the following characteristics:

- focused on their goals,
- willingness to be examined on their accomplishments,
- high interest in improving their skills,
- positive attitude toward their work,
- being on time and respect for deadlines, and
- flexibility in new or changing situations.

"The best way to learn is by doing.
The only way to build a strong work ethic
is getting your hands dirty."
Alex Spanos

Doing your best

If the employee work ethic is endangering the quality or the reputation of the company, employers should be looking for new employees. Characteristics of employees who want to do their best will generally include the following:

1. **Core Values:** They will establish personal core values for their work and set personal standards for excellence. They commit to the core values of the employer.

2. **Self-discipline:** They will be self-starters and motivate themselves to seek excellence. They are intentional about the quality of their work. They learn how and when to say no.

3. **Flexibility:** They will want to adapt to new or different ways of doing things. They are open to change and learning new skills and abilities.

4. Communication: Such employees communicate clearly and openly within the workplace. They are positive and always focus on solutions rather than on finding someone to blame. They tend to encourage others.

5. Focus: They have learned how to eliminate distractions. They are not bothered by what is unimportant. If an employee is easily distracted it is difficult to produce quality work.

6. Consistency. Hard working employees are regular and consistent. Working hard is always important but employees must be reminded that life and work is not a sprint: it's a marathon. It is normally much better for employees to be at work every day than to be exhausted in mind and body because of frequent fifteen-hour work days.

7. Learning. Good employees never stop learning. They must be allowed to develop and grow.

Diligence should be rewarded by both verbal and monetary encouragement. Excellent results will often be recognized and acclaimed by co-workers, others may even try to copy what good employees are doing. Higher compensation is always appreciated.

> *"Talent is never enough. With few exceptions the best players are the hardest workers."*
> Magic Johnson

LEADERS

Effective leaders are the key to successfully producing high quality products. Strong and effective leadership is the key to implementing quality as a core value and providing products recognized for their excellence.

Employers who want the best results will require the best from their employees. Good leaders set high standards and require conformance to those standards. The leader who accepts mediocrity will get mediocrity. Standards should not be unreasonable, but if leaders accept low standards the company will never achieve product excellence. Excellence cannot be attained in an organization unless it is an established expectation for every employee. Leaders can get the best out of their subordinates, often simply because they ask for it.

A leader who demands little will get little. It is not a disaster if subordinates feel out of their comfort zone. It is often only in that discomfort zone that the mettle of high performing people can be identified and exhibited. But the leader may need to join his team in the trenches. Good leaders hold themselves to the same or higher standards as their subordinates.

See Appendix B for help in training leaders.

You get what you demand.
Demand excellence!

ILLUSTRATION: Toyota

Toyota, a Japanese automotive manufacturer, has long been renowned for its commitment to quality. The company's success story is deeply rooted in its adherence to the principles of continuous improvement and delivering high-quality products.

They pioneered the concept of "lean manufacturing" and implemented a production system that emphasizes the elimination of waste while promoting efficient production methods and continuous improvement (innovation). By focusing on quality at every step of the production process, Toyota aimed to deliver vehicles that exceeded customer expectations.

The company has consistently placed a strong emphasis on customer needs and incorporating their feedback into the design and manufacturing processes. This customer-oriented approach has contributed to the development of vehicles known for their reliability and durability.

The concept of "Kaizen," which means continuous improvement in Japanese, is ingrained in Toyota's culture. Employees at all levels are encouraged to contribute ideas for improvement, fostering a culture of innovation and flexibility. This bottom-up approach empowers employees to take ownership of quality and actively participate in the pursuit of excellence.

In the face of challenges, such as recalls and quality issues that emerged, Toyota's commitment to quality became even more evident. The company responded by implementing comprehensive quality control measures, enhancing communication with customers, and reinforcing its dedication to continuous improvement. Despite setbacks, Toyota's reputation for quality remained in place.

This unwavering commitment to quality and excellence has resulted in strong brand loyalty. Customers today often associate the Toyota brand with reliability and superior product quality. This loyalty has contributed to Toyota's sustained market leadership and its ability to weather industry challenges.[B]

"Nobody gains anything from mediocrity."
Stephen H Berkey

PRACTICAL TIPS

Implementing a quality perspective requires a strategic and encompassing approach. Here are some tips for instilling excellence within your organization:

1. *Executive Leadership.* Demonstrate commitment from the top leadership by consistently communicating the importance of quality and excellence. Integrate quality goals into the overall strategic vision and mission of the organization.

2. *Employee Training.* Provide regular training on quality standards and best practices. Encourage a culture of continuous learning and improvement among employees.

3. *Clear Quality Standards.* Clearly define quality standards and expectations for each department. Ensure employees understand how their roles contribute to the overall quality objectives and the success of the company.

4. *Feedback.* Establish mechanisms for gathering feedback from both employees and customers. Act on feedback to drive continuous improvement.

5. *Recognition.* Implement a recognition and reward system for employees who consistently contribute to quality and excellence. Celebrate achievements and milestones related to quality initiatives.

6. *Quality Teams.* Form cross-functional teams focused on process improvement. Empower teams to identify and implement changes that enhance quality.

7. *Customer-Centric.* Instill a customer-oriented mindset by emphasizing the impact of quality on customer satisfaction. Encourage employees to suggest small or incremental changes to improve efficiency and quality.

8. *Performance Indicators.* Establish measurable indicators related to quality and excellence. Regularly monitor and share performance metrics to track progress.

9. *Quality Audits.* Conduct regular internal audits to assess compliance with quality standards.

10. *Quality Circles.* Form quality circles where employees can discuss and investigate quality-related challenges and issues.

> **"Opportunities are usually disguised as hard work,**
> **so most people don't recognize them."**
> Ann Landers

GROUP DISCUSSION QUESTIONS

1. What do the words quality and excellence mean to you and how are they important in your work?

2. How do you measure your own performance and progress in your work? Can you determine if your work is meeting company standards?

3. What are some of the challenges or obstacles that prevent you from producing quality results?

4. What could leadership do that would help you produce a higher quality product?

5. How do you personally balance your work and personal life without compromising the quality of your work?

6. How do you motivate others to do their best work?

7. How do you handle feedback or correction on your work? What training programs would help you do a better job?

8. How could good or excellent work be more effectively rewarded?

9. Do you learn from your mistakes in your work? Why? Why not?

10. How do you collaborate with others who have different work styles or expectations? What are ways teamwork in our organization could be improved?

11. How do you deal with stress or burnout in your work? What is your biggest source for stress? How could your stress be reduced?

12. Do you have ethical dilemmas in your work? How would you describe these dilemmas? How could these issues be eliminated?

GROUP EXERCISE #1 – The Team Challenge

Objective: Demonstrate the significance of giving your best as a team.

Instructions:

a. Divide employees into teams of equal size and assign each team a complex task or problem to solve (e.g., a puzzle, a brainstorming challenge, a simulated business problem).

b. Set a time limit for completion.

c. Explain the focus is on teamwork, diligence, and doing their best as a group.

d. Encourage open communication, collaboration, and the utilization of each team member's strengths.

e. After the time is up, have each team present their solutions.

f. Facilitate a discussion in which teams can share their experiences, challenges, and lessons learned.

g. Discuss the importance of diligence and giving one's best in achieving team success, and how these values contribute to a positive and high-performing work environment.

h. Identify key takeaways that can be applied to everyday work situations to foster a culture of diligence which produces quality products.

GROUP EXERCISE #2 – The Quality Circle Simulation

Objective: Reinforce the importance of continuous improvement and collaborative problem-solving.

Instructions:

a. Divide employees into small groups, each representing a "Quality Circle."

b. Present a simulated scenario or case study involving a quality-related challenge within the organization.

c. Instruct each Quality Circle to analyze the scenario, identify root causes, and propose solutions to improve quality.

d. After a specified time have groups present their findings and solutions to the larger group.

e. Facilitate a discussion on common themes, best practices, and the role of teamwork in achieving quality products.

GROUP EXERCISE #3 – The Quality Reflection and Storytelling

Objective: Encourage employees to reflect on personal experiences related to quality and excellence.

Instructions:

a. Ask employees to individually reflect on a personal or professional experience where they witnessed the impact of quality or excellence.

b. In small groups, have employees share their stories and discuss the important lessons learned.

c. Each group should identify common themes and extract principles that align with the organization's core values of quality and excellence.

d. Have each group present a summarized version of their discussion to the larger group.

e. Facilitate a broader discussion on the collective insights and their relevance to the organization.

Remember to debrief and facilitate discussions after each exercise to ensure employees understand the lessons learned and can apply them to their work environment effectively.

"Be a yardstick of quality. Some people
aren't used to an environment
where excellence is expected."
Steve Jobs

Chapter 3
Customer-Oriented

*"Your most unhappy customers
are your greatest source of learning."*
Bill Gates

GENERAL

Being customer-oriented refers to a core value that places the customer at the center of an organization's strategies. It requires a business mindset and approach that prioritizes exceeding customer expectations. A customer-oriented company places a strong emphasis on building and maintaining positive customer relationships and delivering exceptional product experiences.

When a company embraces a focus on customer satisfaction, it identifies the customer as being the lifeblood of its success and shapes the company culture. The belief is that customer satisfaction and loyalty are critical to long-term success. If this is a core value, you will invest in understanding your target audience, their preferences, pain points, and aspirations. This knowledge will then be used to tailor products, services, and experiences that resonate with customers by solving problems, meeting needs, or adding value to their lives.

Customer feedback is actively sought and utilized to refine products and services and drive continuous improvement and innovation. The company should leverage customer data and insights to identify trends in order to create innovative solutions in the hope of creating competitive advantage.

"The customer's perception is your reality."
Kate Zabriskie

KEY ASPECTS

Being customer-oriented can be categorized as follows:

1. Customer Understanding

A customer-oriented organization invests in gaining a significant and deep understanding of its customers. This includes gathering data, conducting market research, and employing tools and techniques to develop comprehensive customer profiles.

2. Customer Satisfaction

Customer satisfaction is a key performance indicator. The company will strive consistently to deliver products and services that meet and exceed customer expectations. Thus, it is necessary to measure customer satisfaction through surveys, feedback mechanisms, and other methods that help identify areas that need improvement.

3. Customer Engagement

Customer-centric organizations often engage with their customers to foster strong relationships. They provide open and transparent communication channels, seek feedback, and respond to customer inquiries and concerns promptly. Damon Richards said, "Your customer doesn't care how much you know until they know how much you care."

4. Personalization

Some companies may desire to deliver personalized experiences. This involves tailoring products, services, and communications to specific customer preferences and needs.

5. Empowered Employees

Training and support is provided to ensure employees have the necessary skills and knowledge to understand and directly respond to customer needs.

These characteristics collectively contribute to a customer-oriented culture, where the customer's needs and satisfaction are at the forefront of decision-making, strategies, and operations. Satisfied customers become product and brand advocates, spreading positive word-of-mouth recommendations and influencing others to choose the company's products or services.

> *"There is only one boss. The customer!*
> *And he can fire everybody in the company*
> *from the chairman on down, simply*
> *by spending his money somewhere else."*
> Sam Walton

KEY STRATEGIES

Customer research and understanding is the key to being customer-oriented. Adequate time and money must be invested in market research, data analysis, and customer feedback mechanisms to gain insights into customer needs and preferences.

Some companies will find it necessary to perform customer journey mapping. This requires mapping out the entire customer journey, from initial contact to post-sales support for the purpose of identifying pain points. It can be beneficial to optimize each stage of the customer journey to ensure a seamless, personalized, and consistent experience across all aspects of the company.

Communication is extremely important. The significance of customer-centricity must be promoted to employees at all levels. It must be integrated into the company's values, mission, and vision statements. The purpose is to empower employees to prioritize customer needs. The employer must provide employees with the training and tools necessary to deliver the desired exceptional service.

This core value requires that you establish key performance indicators related to satisfaction scores, retention rates, repeat purchase rates, and referral rates. You should regularly track and analyze these metrics to measure the effectiveness of your customer-oriented initiatives and identify areas for improvement.

"The key is to set realistic customer expectations and then not to just meet them, but to exceed them — preferably in unexpected and helpful ways."
Richard Branson

ILLUSTRATION: Amazon

One notable success story that highlights the importance of being customer-oriented is the transformation of amazon.com. Initially founded as an online bookstore, Amazon now has evolved into one of the world's largest and most successful e-commerce companies.

Amazon's success can be attributed in large part to its relentless focus on customer-centricity. From the beginning, Bezos envisioned Amazon as "the Earth's most customer-oriented company." This vision has guided Amazon's strategies, operations, and innovations, leading to exceptional growth and customer loyalty.

One key aspect of Amazon's customer-oriented approach is its commitment to delivering a seamless and convenient shopping experience. The company invested heavily in developing advanced technology, logistics infrastructure, and robust supply chains to ensure fast and reliable product delivery. Amazon Prime, a subscription service offering expedited shipping and additional benefits, was introduced to further enhance customer satisfaction and loyalty.

Amazon also revolutionized the concept of customer reviews, enabling customers to share their experiences and opinions about products. This empowered shoppers with valuable insights from their peers, aiding them in making informed purchasing decisions. By actively encouraging and leveraging customer feedback, Amazon continuously improves its offerings, addresses shortcomings, and enhances customer satisfaction.

Amazon's approach extends to its personalized recommendations. By analyzing customer data, purchase history, and browsing behavior, Amazon employs sophisticated algorithms to provide tailored product recommendations to individual customers. This level of personalization not only enhances the customer experience but also drives increased sales and customer loyalty.

The success of Amazon's customer-centricity is evident in its market dominance and financial performance. The company's relentless focus on meeting customer needs has cultivated a fiercely loyal customer base, with millions of customers relying on Amazon for their shopping needs. This has translated into significant revenue growth and market share expansion across various product categories.[c]

> *"The goal as a company is to have customer service that is not just the best, but legendary."*
> Sam Walton

PRACTICAL TIPS

Here are some tips for implementing this core value in your organization:

1. *Leadership.* Demonstrate commitment by having senior executives promote the core value at every opportunity.

2. *Employee Training.* Provide regular training sessions to educate employees.

3. *Feedback.* Implement easy-to-use mechanisms for gathering customer feedback (surveys, reviews, etc.). Establish key performance indicators (KPIs) related to customer satisfaction.

4. *Empowerment.* Empower frontline employees to make decisions that prioritize customer satisfaction and encourage them to take ownership of customer issues and directly provide solutions.

5. *Communication.* Share customer success stories internally to inspire and reinforce the importance of customer satisfaction. Continually reinforce the customer-oriented vision through internal communications, meetings, and training sessions.

6. *Collaboration.* Encourage collaboration among different departments to ensure a seamless customer experience.

7. *Technology*. Leverage technology to streamline processes and enhance the overall customer experience.

8. *Decision-making*. Integrate customer feedback into the decision-making process.

9. Flexibility. Be willing to consider strategies based on changing customer needs and market dynamics.

GROUP DISCUSSION QUESTIONS

1. In your opinion why should our company prioritize and value its customers? What do we have to gain? What are the benefits?

2. What does being customer-oriented mean to you personally?

3. Share an example of a time when you had a positive customer experience. What made it memorable and how did it influence your perception of that company?

4. How do you think a customer-oriented approach could contribute to building long-term customer satisfaction?

5. What role does effective communication play in producing a customer-oriented work environment?

6. How can employees ensure that they are effectively listening to and understanding customer needs?

7. Do you think being customer oriented can drive innovation? Why? Why not?

8. Can you think of any examples where customer feedback led to significant product or service improvements?

9. What obstacles does our company face in its efforts to become more customer-oriented? How could these challenges be overcome?

10. How could our company better gather and leverage customer feedback to enhance the customer satisfaction?

11. How could the company measure and evaluate its customer-oriented performance?

12. What is the role of leadership in a customer-oriented culture?

QUESTION FOR MANAGEMENT GROUP: In your view, what are the key steps that our organization should take to embed a customer-oriented mindset into our corporate culture, and how can employees contribute to this process?

EXERCISE #1 – Customer Journey Mapping

a. Divide the employees into small groups and assign each group a specific customer segment or persona.

b. Ask each group to map out the customer journey, starting from the initial interaction with the company to post-purchase interactions.

c. Encourage the groups to analyze each touchpoint and identify pain points and areas where the customer experience could be enhanced.

d. After the exercise, have each group present their customer journey maps and facilitate a discussion on common themes, opportunities, and potential solutions to improve the customer experience.

e. Summarize the key insights and action steps that the organization can take to become more customer-oriented based on the exercise.

EXERCISE #2 – Role-Play Scenarios

a. Create different customer scenarios that employees commonly encounter in their roles (e.g., handling a complaint, providing product recommendations, resolving a service issue).

b. Divide the employees into small groups and assign each group a scenario to role-play.

c. Instruct the groups to act out the scenario, with one person playing the role of the customer and the other(s) representing the company.

d. After each role-play, facilitate a debriefing session where participants discuss what went well, areas for improvement, and how the interaction could have been more customer-oriented.

e. Encourage participants to share their insights, strategies, and techniques for delivering exceptional customer experiences.

EXERCISE #3 – Customer Feedback Analysis

a. Provide employees with a sample of real customer feedback, such as online reviews, survey responses, or support tickets.

b. Divide the employees into small groups and distribute the customer feedback among the groups.

c. Instruct the groups to analyze the feedback, identify common themes, and discuss the implications for the organization.

d. Encourage the groups to brainstorm actionable steps based on the feedback to improve the customer experience.

e. Facilitate a group discussion where each group shares their findings, insights, and proposed solutions.

f. Summarize the key takeaways from the exercise and discuss how the organization can effectively leverage customer feedback to drive improvements.

Remember to debrief and facilitate discussions after each exercise to ensure employees understand the lessons learned and can apply them to their work environment effectively.

"The price of success is hard work, dedication to the job at hand, and the determination that whether we win or lose, we have applied the best of ourselves to the task at hand."
Vince Lombardi

Chapter 4
Results-Oriented

"Results are gained by exploiting opportunities,
not by solving problems."
Peter Drucker

GENERAL

Being a company that is results-oriented generally means everyone is focused on measurable financial success. It requires setting clear goals and objectives and dedicating efforts to accomplish them. This core value emphasizes a mindset of accountability, continuous improvement, and a strong commitment to bottom line financial results. It is about fostering a culture where individuals and teams are driven by achieving concrete outcomes.

At its core, being results-oriented requires setting specific measurable goals. These goals provide clarity and direction for measuring success. They enable employees to align their efforts toward achieving the desired outcomes. This core value increases the importance of defining measurable goals that can be regularly reported in order to evaluate success.

Being results-oriented encourages individuals and teams to take ownership and be accountable for their work. It promotes a sense of responsibility for delivering on commitments and meeting deadlines. Having specific financial goals encourages employees to take a proactive approach to their work. Employees are encouraged to seek solutions and take initiative to overcome challenges that may arise because they understand the impact on results.

Continuous improvement in both company and personal performance is a significant aspect of being results-oriented. It involves analyzing outcomes, learning from successes and failures, and adapting strategies to improve results. A growth mindset helps foster innovation and encourages employees to explore new ideas that can produce improved results. Ultimately, a results-oriented culture is about enhancing efficiency, increased competitiveness, and overall financial success.

> *"The way to get started is to*
> *quit talking and begin doing."*
> Walt Disney

KEY ASPECTS

Being results-oriented requires setting clear and measurable goals that align with the organization's objectives. In most companies, goals are related to company profitability, particularly if the company is large and listed on a stock exchange. Thus, proactive behaviors and initiatives are expected and rewarded. There tends to be a bias on action rather than mere planning and analysis.

Results-oriented organizations rely on data and evidence to make informed decisions and track progress. They emphasize collecting, analyzing, and utilizing relevant information to assess performance. The pursuit of continuous learning and employee improvement is a natural result in this type of culture and environment.

Efficiency and effectiveness are highly valued. There is a focus on optimizing resources, eliminating wasteful practices, and streamlining processes in order to maximize productivity. The focus is on the end result rather than interim activities. The company culture is about winning the end-game There may not be great concern about secondary periphery issues. This can sometimes lead to problems because not enough attention is given to all parts of the operation.

Ultimately the best results-oriented strategies produce adaptability and flexibility in response to changing circumstances. This fosters a collaborative environment in which individuals and teams work together toward shared objectives. Effective collaboration and teamwork can leverage diverse perspectives which will result in improved results.

Ultimately, being results-oriented focuses the organization on financial objectives, gaining a competitive edge, and creating sustainable value for all parties. It aligns effort with strategic goals, allowing organizations to navigate challenges, seize opportunities, and achieve meaningful outcomes in a very competitive business landscape.

> *"Results are the only proof of ability."*
> John Wooden

ILLUSTRATION: Netflix

A business success story that illustrates the importance of being results-oriented is the transformation of Netflix from a DVD rental company to a global streaming powerhouse.

In the early 2000s, Netflix faced intense competition in the DVD rental market, particularly from Blockbuster, the dominant player at the time. Recognizing the shifting landscape of media consumption, Netflix's leadership, led by Reed Hastings, decided to refine their business model and embrace digital streaming for their future.

The transformation process required a strong commitment to bottom line results. Netflix set a clear goal of becoming the leading provider of online streaming content. They focused on developing a robust technology infrastructure, securing content licensing agreements, and creating a seamless user experience.

One of the key aspects of Netflix's results-oriented approach was their data-driven decision-making. They analyzed user behavior, viewing patterns, and preferences to tailor their content offerings, recommendations, and user interface. This data-driven approach allowed them to continuously refine their platform and deliver a personalized and engaging streaming experience.

Netflix also demonstrated adaptability and a willingness to take risks. In 2011, they announced a controversial decision to split their DVD rental service into a separate brand called Qwikster. This decision resulted in significant backlash from customers. Responding quickly to the negative feedback, Netflix reevaluated their decision, scrapped the

Qwikster plan, and apologized to their customers. This incident showcased their responsiveness and ability to make course corrections based on customer feedback and market dynamics.

As a result of their results-oriented strategies, Netflix achieved remarkable success. They rapidly expanded their streaming service globally, investing heavily in original content production to differentiate themselves in the competitive streaming market. This led to massive subscriber growth, with Netflix becoming the dominant player in the streaming industry, surpassing 200 million subscribers worldwide.[D]

> *"The best way to predict the future*
> *is to create it."*
> Peter Drucker

PRACTICAL TIPS

Implementing a results-oriented culture involves aligning the organization's actions and strategies with the achievement of real tangible outcomes. Here are some simple tips to implement a strategy of being results-oriented:

1. Clearly define and promote organizational objectives results that align with the overall mission.

2. Communicate company goals throughout the organization, ensuring that everyone understands their role in achieving the results.

3. Establish measurable performance statistics that align with organizational goals and regularly measure and assess performance against these metrics.

4. Conduct regular performance reviews that focus on results and outcomes. Provide personal constructive feedback based on achievement of goals and key results.

5. Encourage employees to prioritize high-impact activities that directly contribute to desired results. Discourage unnecessary or low-impact strategies that do not align with organizational goals.

6. Foster a culture of accountability in which individuals take ownership of their responsibilities.

7. Establish regular communication channels to update everyone on department and company progress.

8. Celebrate milestones and successes. Encourage a positive culture focused on results. Implement a reward system that acknowledges and celebrates achievements that are tied directly to the accomplishment of key results and goals.

9. Instill a culture of continuous examination and analysis in which teams regularly evaluate processes and strategies.

10. Invest in the development of employees' skills and capabilities to enhance their ability to contribute to results.

GROUP DISCUSSION QUESTIONS

1. Why do you think it is important for our organization to have a clear focus on achieving goals and objectives?

2. How do you think being results-oriented contributes to the success and growth of our organization?

3. Share examples of situations where the absence of a mindset on results hindered our progress or impacted our performance?

4. Do you think being results-oriented aligns with our organization's mission and vision?

5. How do you think being results-oriented can drive innovation and creativity within our organization? How can we encourage innovation?

6. How does being results-oriented affect our relationships with customers? Does it help or hinder customer satisfaction?

7. Does our results-oriented approach impact employee engagement and motivation? What improvements are needed?

8. What challenges or barriers do we face in developing a results-oriented culture within our organization?

9. What specific behaviors should leaders practice in order to reinforce the importance of being results-oriented?

10. How can we strike a balance between short-term results and long-term strategic objectives?

11. What role does company compensation and financial rewards play in the successful maintenance of a results-oriented atmosphere?

12. What steps can we take as a company to embed the corporate core value of being results-oriented into our everyday work culture?

"There are no secrets to success.
It is the result of preparation,
hard work, and learning from failure."
Colin Powell

EXERCISE #1 – Case Study Analysis

Divide employees into small groups and provide each group with a case study that highlights a situation in which a results-oriented approach led to significant organizational success or in which a lack of results-oriented mindset caused poor results. The groups should analyze the case study, discuss the key factors that contributed to the outcome, and identify lessons learned. Each group can then present their findings to the larger group, followed by a discussion on the importance of being results-oriented and how it can drive organizational success.

EXERCISE #2 – Results-Oriented Goal Setting

In this exercise, guide employees through the process of setting results-oriented goals. Begin by explaining the characteristics of SMART goals (Specific, Measurable, Achievable, Relevant, Time-bound). Then, divide employees into small groups and ask them to identify a specific work-related goal that aligns with the organization's objectives. Encourage participants to make the goal measurable and time-bound. After setting the goals, facilitate a discussion on the importance of results-oriented goal setting, how it contributes to individual and organizational success, and the strategies they can use to achieve those goals.

EXERCISE #3 – Results-Oriented Simulation Game

Design a simulation game that requires participants to work together and make decisions to achieve specific results within a given timeframe. The game can simulate a business scenario or a project in which participants must allocate resources, solve problems, and prioritize tasks to achieve desired outcomes. After completing the simulation, facilitate a debriefing session in which participants reflect on the importance of being results-oriented during the game, the challenges they faced, and the strategies they employed to achieve results. Discuss the transferability of those strategies to their real work environment and encourage participants to share their insights.

Remember to debrief and facilitate discussions after each exercise to ensure employees understand the lessons learned and can apply them to their work environment effectively.

> *"Don't lower your expectations*
> *to meet your performance.*
> *Raise your level of performance*
> *to meet your expectations."*
> Ralph Marston

Chapter 5
Innovation

*"Innovation is the ability to see change
as an opportunity, not a threat."*
Steve Jobs

GENERAL

The corporate core value of innovation can be described as the commitment to and belief in creating a culture of creativity and exploration within an organization. It is a mindset that encourages new ideas that bring value to the company.

At its core, innovation is about challenging the status quo, pushing boundaries, and seeking new and better solutions to problems. It requires being open to change and embracing some level of risk. It means encouraging a supportive environment where individuals are empowered to think outside the box and take calculated risks.

A company that prioritizes innovation as a core value believes that creativity is essential for long-term sustainability. The belief is that by instilling an innovative culture, the organization can adapt to evolving market conditions and stay ahead of its competition. It inherently encourages employees to be proactive and forward-thinking, creating an environment that generates new ideas and experimentation.

Innovation as a corporate core value is not limited to technological advancements or product development. It encompasses a broader perspective that encompasses processes, business modeling, customer experiences, and even organizational structure. It encourages a broad approach to generating improvements and breakthroughs in all aspects of the business.

Innovation inherently emphasizes the importance of flexibility and adaptability in a constantly changing business environment. It must accept failure as a learning experience and view setbacks as stepping stones toward progress and success.

In summary, innovation fosters a culture that celebrates and supports creativity, encourages experimentation, and is in constant search for improvement and growth through new concepts and ideas. In this environment innovation will guide major decision-making. It positions the company for success by creating a dynamic business environment.

> *The real sign of success is not knowledge but understanding combined with innovation.*

CHARACTERISTICS OF INNOVATION

This core value encompasses characteristics that exist to some extent in all companies. However, innovation as a core value demands openness to change and a willingness to challenge existing norms and practices. It encourages employees to embrace change and quickly adapt to new technologies or market trends. Innovative companies are continually seeking new and better ways to deliver their products. Thus, it nurtures imagination, divergent thinking, and the exploration of unconventional solutions. Crazy ideas are not dismissed without some degree of consideration.

Innovation inherently requires taking calculated risks and challenging the status quo. It means individuals must generate the courage to step outside their comfort zones and embrace uncertainty. They must consider opportunities that may not have guaranteed outcomes. This is not always easy.

Innovation values experimentation and learning from both successes and failures. It encourages a mindset that sees failures as opportunities to grow and learn. Failures are considered valuable lessons that can lead to new breakthroughs.

Innovation is more likely to thrive in an environment where collaboration and cross-functional integration are encouraged. It recognizes that different perspectives, expertise, and experiences can lead to more innovative and improved outcomes. Thus, teamwork and knowledge sharing are encouraged throughout the organization.

Embracing innovation can future-proof a business! By being prepared for emerging trends and changing customer expectations, executives position their companies to lead rather than react.

In summary, innovation enables companies to be out in front of technological advancements, market disruptions, and changing customer preferences. Effective innovation can give businesses a competitive edge by differentiating them from competitors, creating unique offerings, and capturing new market opportunities. It allows companies to stay ahead of the curve and adapt to changing customer demands. Innovative companies can produce a stimulating work environment that attracts and retains top talent.

Creativity is the fuel of Innovation.
It converts threats into opportunities.

ILLUSTRATION: Warby Parker

Warby Parker is an eyewear company that was founded in 2010 by four friends who were frustrated by the high cost of prescription glasses. They identified a gap in the market and saw an opportunity to disrupt the traditional eyewear industry by offering affordable stylish glasses directly to consumers.

What sets Warby Parker apart is its innovative approach to the eyewear industry. They introduced the concept of "try before you buy" by offering a home try-on program. Customers can select up to five frames online, have them delivered to their homes, and try them out for free. This approach eliminated the need for customers to visit physical stores.

Warby Parker also implemented a socially conscious business model. For every pair of glasses sold, they donate a pair to someone in need through their "Buy a Pair, Give a Pair" program. This not only resonated with customers but also differentiated the company in the market, appealing to socially conscious consumers.

Through their innovative business model Warby Parker quickly gained traction and disrupted the eyewear industry. They challenged the traditional distribution channels dominated by retail stores and provided an affordable and convenient alternative to consumers. By cutting out the middlemen and utilizing an online platform, they were able to offer high-quality fashionable eyewear at a fraction of the cost.

Warby Parker's success story showcases the power of innovation for a small unknown company. By identifying a market gap, reimagining the purchasing process, and aligning their business model with social awareness, they were able to create unique value and gain a loyal customer base. Today they have expanded and offer sunglasses, contact lenses, and they now also have physical retail stores.

This example highlights how innovation can level the playing field for smaller companies, enabling them to disrupt established industries and carve out their own success. It emphasizes the importance of identifying unmet customer needs, taking a customer-oriented approach, and being willing to challenge conventional practices to drive business growth.[E]

"Innovation is the calling card
of the future."
Anna Eshoo

PRACTICAL TIPS

1. Access: Encourage open communication and idea-sharing by adopting an open-door policy. Create an environment where employees feel comfortable approaching their managers or leaders.

2. Feedback: Encourage employees to provide constructive feedback on all aspects of the business. Implement an idea management system that allows employees to submit ideas.

3. Space: Provide informal spaces or platforms for employees to share ideas casually. This could be through dedicated brainstorming sessions, virtual collaboration tools, or just informal gatherings.

4. Time: Set aside regular "innovation hours" or designated days where employees can focus on brainstorming, experimenting, and developing new ideas.

5. Acknowledge and Reward: Acknowledge and celebrate all employees who contribute innovative ideas. Provide incentives and rewards for new ideas that produce positive results.

6. Networking: Encourage and help employees attend industry conferences, seminars, or workshops related to their field of work.

7. Advocates: Identify and appoint "Innovation Advocates" within the organization. These individuals act as advocates for innovation, encouraging and inspiring innovative thinking. They can also be sounding boards for new ideas.

> *"Innovation is not just about new technology;*
> *it's about new ideas, new ways of thinking,*
> *and new approaches to problem-solving."*
> Barack Obama

GROUP DISCUSSION QUESTIONS

1. What does innovation mean to you, and why would it be important in our organization?

2. Can you recall a time when innovation played a significant role in the success of a project or initiative? How did it make a difference?

3. How do you think the core value of innovation aligns with our organization's overall mission?

4. What are some potential risks or challenges associated with embracing innovation? How could such risks be minimized?

5. How might a culture of innovation impact employee morale? Can you provide examples?

6. What are some potential barriers to innovation within our organization, and how can we overcome them?

7. What role can employees play in promoting a culture of innovation within our organization?

8. How can innovation contribute to enhancing the customer experience or drive customer satisfaction?

9. How could we encourage employees to bring innovative ideas and creativity to management?

10. What resources and support do employees need in order to feel empowered or comfortable in contributing innovative ideas?

11. How can we create an environment in which failure is seen as a learning opportunity and not a deterrent to innovation?

12. How could we leverage emerging technologies to drive innovation in our organization?

> *"Innovation is the lifeblood of any business.*
> *It's the engine of growth and progress."*
> Larry Page

EXERCISE #1 – Innovation Case Studies

Divide the employees into small groups and provide them with case studies of real-world companies that have successfully embraced innovation. Each group should analyze the case study, identify the innovative practices or strategies employed by the company and discuss the impact of those innovations on the company's success. Afterward, reconvene as a larger group to share and discuss the key learning concepts from each case study.

EXERCISE #2 – Innovation Challenge

Organize an innovation challenge in which groups of employees are tasked with solving a specific problem or coming up with an innovative solution related to a current business challenge faced by the company. Provide them with guidelines, resources, and a designated time frame to brainstorm ideas and develop proposals. Each group should present their solutions to a panel of judges or the larger employee group.

EXERCISE #3 – Innovation Workshop

Conduct an interactive innovation workshop where employees actively engage in various creative thinking techniques and brainstorming exercises. Teach different methodologies. Guide participants through exercises that encourage them to generate new ideas, challenge assumptions, and explore creative approaches. By experiencing firsthand the power of creative thinking and idea generation, employees gain a deeper understanding of how innovation can drive positive change.

Remember to debrief and facilitate discussions after each exercise to ensure employees understand the lessons learned and can apply them to their work environment effectively.

"Creativity is thinking up new things.
Innovation is doing new things."
Theodore Levitt

Chapter 6
Teamwork

"Teamwork makes the dream work."
John C. Maxwell

GENERAL

The core value of teamwork means the organization is committed to encouraging collaborative efforts among individuals. It encompasses the concept that when employees work together as a team, share their skills, knowledge, and resources, they can produce highly effective results. The belief is that the organization can achieve greater outcomes when employees are collaborating together than when they work independently or separately.

The concept of teamwork involves the recognition that ultimate success is not solely dependent on individual efforts, but on the collective strength and synergy of the group. It involves creating an environment where employees are encouraged to collaborate, cooperate, and actively engage with each other to achieve their goals. Teamwork requires mutual respect, open communication, and a shared sense of purpose.

Effective teamwork involves clear and open communication, active listening, and the willingness to share ideas and expertise. It requires a culture of trust in which individuals feel comfortable relying on their teammates and supporting one another. Collaboration becomes a natural part of the work process, leading to increased innovation and improved problem-solving.

Teamwork as a core value extends beyond the individual team and should permeate the entire culture of the organization. It encourages breaking down department walls that automatically exist and adopting cross-functional working relationships. It intends to create a sense of unity and common purpose among employees at all levels.

> *"If everyone is moving forward together,*
> *then success takes care of itself."*
> Henry Ford

CHARACTERISTICS and ASPECTS

Teamwork encompasses various characteristics and aspects that contribute to its effectiveness:

1. Collaboration: Teamwork involves individuals working together toward a shared goal, actively collaborating and pooling their skills, abilities, and knowledge.

2. Communication: Effective communication is crucial. It involves sharing information, expressing ideas clearly, and providing constructive feedback in order to encourage collaborative efforts.

3. Trust: Trust may be the foundational component of a successful team. It allows team members to rely on and have confidence in the abilities, integrity, and intentions of other team members. It creates a safe environment in which employees can be vulnerable, take risks, and openly share their perspectives. The best environments are those in which team members can argue their own positions openly without concern that another team member will take personal offense because they do not like the idea.

4. Respect: If trust is the fundamental component of teamwork, then mutual respect among team members becomes a requirement of that trust. Respect requires recognizing and appreciating the diverse backgrounds, experiences, and particularly the ideas and contributions of each individual. This characteristic is much easier to achieve when the primary or only goal of all employees is the achievement of a specific common goal.

5. Accountability: Teamwork involves shared accountability, where all team members take responsibility for the team's results. It involves holding oneself and others accountable for meeting commitments.

6. Cooperation: Cooperation is necessary to work harmoniously together, setting aside personal differences or interests for the benefit of the team and its objectives. This is easier to accomplish when team members have a common objective.

7. Flexibility: Success is far easier when the team atmosphere supports flexibility and adaptability. Achieving objectives is improved when everyone is open to different ideas, perspectives, and approaches. Leaders need team members who are willing to adjust their own viewpoints and work methods as needed to achieve team goals.

8. Conflict: Effective teamwork involves the ability to manage and resolve conflicts quickly and constructively.

9. Recognition: Recognizing individual and team achievements is an important aspect of teamwork. Acknowledging and appreciating the contributions of all team members boosts morale and motivation.

In summary, teamwork is often crucial for organizations that succeed in today's dynamic business landscape. It can be the foundation of a high-performing organization. Communication plays a vital role in implementing and reinforcing teamwork, as clear and consistent messaging about the work is essential. Ultimately, by reinforcing the importance of teamwork, organizations can create an environment that inspires collaboration, innovation, and high performance, leading to sustainable growth and success.

> *"Teamwork is the ability to work together toward a common vision. It is the ability to direct individual accomplishments toward organizational objectives. It is the fuel that allows common people to attain uncommon results."*
> Andrew Carnegie

ILLUSTRATION: SpaceX

One notable business success story that illustrates the importance of teamwork is the story of SpaceX, the aerospace company founded by Elon Musk. SpaceX's achievement of becoming the first privately funded company to successfully launch, orbit, and recover a spacecraft, as well as the first to send a spacecraft to the International Space Station (ISS), illustrates the power of teamwork.

SpaceX's success can be attributed in part to its strong emphasis on collaboration and teamwork throughout its organization. Their particular teamwork-driven approach centered around six concepts:

1. Vision: Elon Musk initially sets a clear and ambitious vision for SpaceX: to revolutionize space technology and make human life multi-planetary. This vision serves as a unifying force that rallies employees around a common purpose.

2. Collaboration: SpaceX fosters a culture encouraging employees from various disciplines to work together. Engineers, technicians, and scientists collaborate closely, breaking down traditional departmental boundaries to achieve cross-functional objectives.

3. Problem-Solving: SpaceX teams work together to identify challenges and examine designs and processes. This approach allows for rapid innovation and continuous improvement.

4. Environment: Teamwork at SpaceX thrives because employees feel they are empowered. Open communication, idea sharing, and respectful feedback are not only encouraged, they are required. Team members feel comfortable challenging the status quo and taking calculated risks.

5. Standards: SpaceX sets high standards for performance and holds team members accountable. Each employee understands his role in the success of the mission and is expected to take personal responsibility for their contributions.

6. Learning Culture: SpaceX promotes a learning culture that values continuous personal growth and development. Teams learn from

failures and share lessons they learn with others. This enables them to continuously refine their technologies.

Not only did SpaceX develop and launch the Falcon 1 and Falcon 9 rockets, but they also successfully landed and reused rocket boosters—a groundbreaking innovation that significantly reduced the cost of space travel. In addition, their collaboration with NASA led to the Dragon spacecraft delivering supplies and astronauts to the ISS.

SpaceX is an example of teamwork pushing the boundaries of what is possible. By encouraging collaboration, embracing a shared vision, and nurturing a culture of innovation and accountability, SpaceX achieved extraordinary accomplishments.[F]

> **"Great things in business are never done by one person.**
> **They're done by a team of people."**
> Steve Jobs

FIVE PRACTICAL TIPS

1. Leaders should serve as role models in leading teams.

2. Clear and frequent communication of the importance of teamwork and its benefits should be a priority.

3. Teams should be encouraged to develop group goals that exceed company objectives.

4. Workshops and employee training classes should focus on teamwork skills. The company should sponsor activities that promote collaboration, trust, and relationship-building (see exercises below).

5. Leaders should regularly evaluate the effectiveness of their teams. Feedback from employees should be regularly solicited.

> **"Unity is strength . . . when there is teamwork and**
> **collaboration, wonderful things can be achieved."**
> Mattie Stepanek

GROUP DISCUSSION QUESTIONS

1. Why do you think teamwork is considered a critical core value in our company? What benefits does it offer?

2. Share an example from your own experience where teamwork made a significant difference in achieving a goal.

3. What potential obstacles do you see or experience when working in teams? How could these problems be reduced or overcome?

4. In your opinion, how does teamwork enhance creativity and innovation within our organization? Cite examples.

5. What role do you think effective communication plays in successful teamwork? How can we improve communication within our teams?

6. Can you think of any real-life examples where a lack of teamwork negatively impacted a company project? What lessons can we learn?

7. How can we strike a balance between individual accountability and collective responsibility in a team setting?

8. What strategies can we employ to ensure that all team members actively contribute and feel valued as both an individual and a team?

9. Would you feel "safe" in making a "risky" decision in your present job? Why? Why not?

10. Would additional cross-functional cooperation improve overall organizational performance? Why?

11. How can we leverage technology to enhance teamwork and collaboration in our organization?

12. Phil Jackson said, "*The strength of the team is each individual member. The strength of each member is the team.*" How would you explain the meaning of this quote?

EXERCISE #1 – Team Building Escape Room

Engage employees in an interactive team-building exercise such as an escape room. Divide employees into small teams and challenge them to solve puzzles and complete tasks within a specified time frame to "escape" the room. This exercise promotes teamwork, communication, problem-solving, and collaboration as teams must work together to find solutions and achieve a common goal. Afterwards, facilitate a discussion where participants can reflect on how effective teamwork contributed to their success or failure.

EXERCISE #2 – The Tower of Excellence

a. Divide employees into small groups and provide each group with a set of materials (e.g., building blocks, cups, index cards).

b. Explain that the goal is to construct the tallest and most stable tower using the provided materials within a specified time limit.

> ALTERNATIVE: Require teams to build the <u>tallest</u> freestanding structure using spaghetti sticks, tape, string, and a marshmallow (or materials from your organization).

c. Emphasize the importance of teamwork and doing their best to achieve the desired outcome.

d. Set a time limit for the construction phase.

e. After the time is up, have each group present their tower and measure the height and stability.

f. Facilitate a group discussion on the strategies employed, challenges faced, and the importance of teamwork in achieving success.

g. Reflect on how these values can be applied in the workplace and discuss the impact of individual and collective efforts on the overall outcome.

EXERCISE #3 – Team Simulation

Use team simulation exercises that replicate real-life scenarios to emphasize the importance of teamwork. This can include activities such as a survival scenario, a business simulation, or a project management exercise. Provide teams with a simulated challenge or task and ask them to work together to overcome obstacles, make decisions, and achieve specific objectives. After the simulation, facilitate a discussion where participants can reflect on the impact of teamwork on their performance, challenges faced, and key concepts they learned.

Remember to debrief and facilitate discussions after each exercise to ensure employees understand the lessons learned and can apply them to their work environment effectively.

"Alone we can do so little;
together we can do so much."
Helen Keller

Chapter 7
Employee Development

"The greatest asset of a company is its people,
and the greatest investment a company
can make is in developing its people."
John C. Maxwell

GENERAL

Employee development is a term that describes an organization's commitment to encouraging and enhancing the knowledge, skills, and overall growth of its employees. It requires providing learning opportunities, training programs, and resources to support employees in both their professional and personal development.

This core value recognizes that the success of a company is deeply intertwined with the development and well-being of its workforce. It encompasses various aspects such as, skill enhancement, continuous learning, career advancement, and personal growth.

In prioritizing employee development the objective of the company is to develop talent in its workforce to outperform its competition. It will often include implementing training programs, mentorship initiatives, performance feedback, and providing various resources for personal and ongoing learning and development. The objective is to provide the employees with the necessary tools and support to increase their abilities and skills in order to help them become more engaged, motivated, and productive contributors to the organization.

In summary, this core value reflects a commitment to invest in the well-being of employees. It provides them with opportunities to enhance their skills and abilities. It creates a work culture that promotes real engagement in the work and a desire for ongoing learning and growth, both personal and professional.

> *"Train people well enough so they can leave,*
> *treat them well enough so*
> *they don't want to."*
> Richard Branson

KEY ASPECTS

Employee training and development emphasizes a culture in which employees are provided with opportunities to expand their knowledge and stay updated on industry trends and developments. It focuses on developing and enhancing employees' specific job-related skills to improve their performance and contribute to both their personal professional growth and the bottom line of the company.

Employee development values the importance of providing career pathways. It includes initiatives that enable employees to advance in their careers by recognizing the importance of the employees' personal growth and well-being. This can include professional skills, work-life balance programs, or even wellness activities.

One company objective is to identify high-potential employees and nurture their talents through targeted development programs. It involves identifying and investing in talented individuals who have the potential for leadership and the desire to improve and advance. Mentorship and coaching may be part of this development process.

Resources will be required! The company must be prepared to allocate resources, both financial and non-financial, to support employee development. This will necessarily include training programs, educational opportunities, technology tools, or other resources that aid in employee growth and skill improvement.

Regular performance feedback is a critical aspect of any company culture but it is particularly pivotal for employee development. It can include providing coaching and personal guidance to help employees reach their full potential.

Recognizing and rewarding employee growth is an important aspect of this core value. This may include public recognition, promotions, bonuses, or other incentives for rewarding achievement that results in positive contributions to the organization.

In summary, this corporate core value is very important for long-term company success. Employee growth increases the employer's ability to adapt to market dynamics and drive innovation. It enhances the ability to attract and retain top talent, enhancing the ability to be innovative. A focus on the skills of the workforce recognizes that investing in employees' development leads to happy and satisfied employees.

Ultimately employee development empowers individuals, strengthens the organization, and positions it for sustainable growth in a competitive business environment.

> *"Take care of your employees,*
> *and they will take care of your business."*
> Richard Branson

ILLUSTRATIONS

Google

Google has long been renowned for its emphasis on employee development and creating a culture of continuous learning. The company's "20% time" policy is a notable example of how they foster employee growth and innovation. This policy allows employees to spend 20% of their working hours on personal projects that interest them, even if those projects are outside of their core responsibilities. This initiative has led to the creation of several innovative products and features, including Gmail and Google News.

Another noteworthy aspect of Google's employee development is their focus on mentorship and coaching. The company pairs employees with experienced mentors who provide guidance and support for skill-building and career advancement. This mentorship culture fosters a sense of community and collaboration, enabling employees to learn from seasoned professionals and grow both personally and professionally.

The company's dedication to nurturing talent, encouraging innovation, and providing opportunities for individual growth has resulted in a highly engaged and motivated workforce. This, in turn, has led to the creation of groundbreaking services and high employee retention.[G1]

HubSpot

HubSpot, a smaller software company based in Cambridge, Massachusetts, places a strong emphasis on employee development and growth. It has played a significant role in their success and growth as a company. They offer a variety of initiatives to foster a culture of continuous learning and personal growth. One of their notable initiatives is the "HubSpot Academy," an online learning platform that provides free courses and certifications in marketing, sales, and customer service. This initiative allows employees to enhance their skills and knowledge, and also serves as a resource for customers and industry professionals.

In addition the company invests in regular professional development opportunities for its employees. It provides access to industry conferences, workshops, and training programs to keep the workforce up-to-date with the latest trends and best practices. HubSpot encourages employees to attend internal and external training sessions and offers tuition reimbursement for further education and certifications. This commitment to employee growth and development has led to high employee satisfaction and low turnover rates.

By investing in their employees' knowledge and skills, HubSpot has built a highly motivated workforce. This has translated into exceptional customer service, product innovation, and sustainable business growth.[G2]

"Investing in people is the best investment
any company can make."
Sir Richard Branson

PRACTICAL TIPS

1. Encourage employees to explore online courses, industry articles, webinars, podcasts, or TED talks that align with their interests and career goals.

2. Organize regular "lunch and learn" sessions where employees share their particular knowledge and expertise with their colleagues.

3. Encourage employees to learn from each other by establishing peer-to-peer learning initiatives. Encourage cross-team collaboration, where employees can shadow or work with colleagues from different departments to gain exposure to new skills and perspectives.

4. Form book clubs or learning circles in which employees can read and discuss relevant books, articles, or industry publications.

5. Recognize and celebrate employees who actively engage in learning and development activities.

6. Create project teams focused on specific skills or areas of interest.

7. Organize collaboration days in which employees from different teams or departments can come together to share knowledge, collaborate on projects, or learn from each other's expertise.

8. Create an internal learning resources library where employees can access a collection of books, videos, online courses, and other materials relevant for their professional development.

"To win in the marketplace,
you must first win in the workplace."
Doug Conant

GROUP DISCUSSION QUESTIONS

1. Do you think employee development and growth is essential for the long-term success of our company? Why? Why not?

2. How does employee development and growth contribute to employee engagement and job satisfaction?

3. How do employee development initiatives impact productivity and overall organizational performance? Explain.

4. What are the potential consequences of neglecting employee development?

5. Is employee development important in your department? Where in the company is it most/least important?

6. What role does employee development play in our company in building a strong leadership pipeline?

7. How do employee development programs enhance employee loyalty and commitment to the organization?

8. Can you think of any strategies for measuring the impact and effectiveness of employee development programs?

9. How can our company create a culture that encourages and supports continuous learning and development at all levels?

10. Should employees be held accountable for improved skills or additional knowledge in annual performance evaluations? Why? Why not?

11. How can technology and digital platforms be leveraged to enhance employee development and growth in our company?

"The strength of the team is each individual member.
the strength of each member is the team."
Phil Jackson

EXERCISE #1 – Case Study Analysis

Divide employees into small groups and provide each group with a case study that highlights either the negative or the positive impact of employee development and growth on a company. The case study can showcase how a company achieved success (or lack thereof) through investing in employee development initiatives. In their groups, employees should analyze the case study, identify key factors that contributed to the company's performance, and discuss the importance of employee development in achieving desired outcomes. Each group can then present their findings to the larger group, followed by a group discussion on the overall importance of employee development and growth.

EXERCISE #2 – Personal Development Action Plan

In this exercise the employees work individually to create a Personal Development Plan. Provide employees with a template or worksheet that includes sections for them to identify their professional goals, areas for development, and specific actions they can take to grow and improve their skills. Encourage employees to reflect on the importance of personal development for their career growth and overall job satisfaction. After completing their action plans, employees can form small groups to discuss their goals, share insights, and provide feedback to each other.

There are certainly some positive implications of the employee developing this plan, but unless the employee commits to completing the action steps, the actual impact will be relatively small. Take steps consistent with your company culture to get the employee to commit to working the plan. Alternatively, the HR Department could follow up with each employee individually and discuss progress and how they could assist the employee.

EXERCISE #3 – Learning Exchange

Organize a learning exchange session in which employees can share their knowledge, skills, or expertise with their colleagues. Each employee can prepare a short presentation or demonstration on a topic in which they have knowledge and interest. It can be a technical skill, industry trend, or a personal development practice. This exercise allows employees to showcase their own expertise and contribute to the collective learning of the group. After each presentation, encourage open discussions, questions, and feedback.

Remember to debrief and facilitate discussions after each exercise to ensure employees understand the lessons learned and can apply them to their work environment effectively.

*"If you invest in your employees,
they will invest in your business."*
Simon Sinek

Chapter 8
Accountability

*"Accountability is the glue that
ties commitment to results."*
Bob Proctor

GENERAL

The company core value of accountability or responsibility refers to the commitment of individuals and organizations to take ownership of their actions and the resulting outcomes. It involves acknowledging and accepting the consequences, both positive and negative, that arise from personal or corporate decisions.

At its core, accountability entails being answerable for fulfilling assigned tasks and meeting obligations. It goes beyond simply following directives; it involves a proactive mindset to take responsibility and be accountable for results. Individuals who embody this value understand that they play an integral role in the success of the organization and that their actions have a direct impact on its overall success.

In the same way, an organization is accountable for its products, services, guarantees, and promises. It takes responsibility for its business and if something is not right, it must be fixed or made right.

*"You are not only responsible for what you say,
but also for what you do not say."*
Martin Luther

ASPECTS OF ACCOUNTABILITY

Accountability means taking personal responsibility for company promises or commitments. It means being responsible for the quality and consequences of decisions and a commitment to delivering expected results. Accountability and responsibility encompass several key aspects:

Reliability: Being reliable is a crucial aspect of accountability. It means consistently meeting commitments, deadlines, and expectations. Reliable individuals and companies can be trusted to follow through on their responsibilities even when difficulties occur. They are trustworthy. Such organizations will adjust and respond to set-backs and changing circumstances, demonstrating resilience and perseverance in the face of obstacles.

Problem-solving: Individuals and companies who prioritize accountability are often proactive problem solvers. They identify issues and take the initiative to find solutions in order to overcome problems. They approach challenges with a mindset focused on finding solutions, rather than placing blame or avoiding responsibility.

Ethics: Upholding ethical standards and aligning actions with the organization's core values are crucial aspects of accountability. Accountable employees make decisions and act in a manner that promotes trust because they align themselves with the organization's core values, particularly as it relates to integrity and trust.

Learning: Accepting responsibility often means embracing a learning mindset or company culture. Accountability inherently recognizes that mistakes or failures are opportunities for learning and improvement. Individuals and organizations that value accountability understand the importance of continuous learning and development in order to improve their ability to deliver on commitments.

Overall, this core value establishes a culture of trust, reliability, and commitment within an organization, creating a culture that values ownership, transparency, and proactive problem-solving. Being responsible empowers individuals to make decisions and take ownership of their roles in contributing to the overall success and reputation of the company. It allows employees to represent the interests, values, and beliefs of the organization.

Accountability and responsibility are demonstrated when a company shows they stand by their promises. When trust or integrity is missing, all aspects of a company can be impacted. When a company takes ethical ownership of their products, it will positively impact market recognition and their brand. It is much easier to produce quality products and services in such a synergistic workplace environment.

When employees take ownership for delivering high-quality products and meeting business commitments, it leads to satisfied customers who trust and remain loyal to the organization. When individuals hold themselves accountable for company promises, it cultivates an environment of trust and mutual respect in the marketplace.

> *"Responsibility is the price of greatness."*
> Winston Churchill

ILLUSTRATION: Ford Motor Company

One business success story that exemplifies the importance of the corporate core value of accountability and responsibility is the transformation of Ford Motor Company under the leadership of Alan Mulally. In the early 2000s, Ford was facing significant challenges, including financial losses, declining market share, and internal dysfunction. Alan Mulally was appointed as CEO in 2006 and implemented a culture of accountability and responsibility that played a pivotal role in turning the company around.

Mulally established a weekly business review meeting called the "The BPR" (Business Plan Review), which all senior executives were required to attend and report on their respective divisions' progress. This meeting served as a platform for open and transparent communication, with each executive being accountable for their performance and responsible for addressing any issues or challenges.

One notable development that highlighted the value of accountability was the "green, yellow, red" reporting system introduced by Mulally. During the BPR meetings, executives were required to present their progress using a color-coded system. Green indicated everything was on track, yellow indicated potential challenges or risks, and red indicated significant issues that required immediate attention. This system created a culture where executives felt accountable for their divisions' performance and responsible for openly flagging any obstacles or setbacks.

Through this culture Mulally was able to address long-standing issues within the company and foster collaboration among the leadership team. Rather than blaming individuals or departments for problems, the focus was on finding solutions and collectively working toward achieving the company's goals.

As a result of the emphasis on accountability, Ford made significant strides in improving its financial performance and regaining market share. Mulally's leadership and the improved culture played a crucial role in the company's successful turnaround, allowing Ford to avoid the government bailout that other major automakers required during the financial crisis of 2008.[H]

This success story highlights the power of creating a culture where individuals take ownership of their actions while working toward a shared vision of success within the organization.

"Accountability is not an abstract concept;
it's about making a difference and
delivering on what we promise."
Indra Nooyi

PRACTICAL TIPS

The following practical tips and suggestions will help implement accountability into your workplace environment:

1. Clearly define all core values of the organization and communicate them frequently to all employees.

2. Clearly define roles, responsibilities, and expectations for each employee. When individuals understand what is expected of them, they are more likely to take ownership of their work. Include the expectation of being accountable and taking responsibility for actions and results in company job descriptions.

3. Establish a feedback culture in which leaders provide regular feedback to employees regarding their performance.

4. Celebrate instances in which employees have demonstrated exceptional accountability.

5. Honesty and integrity are associated core values. If they are not, consider adding or integrating them into your corporate strategies.

6. Leaders must lead by example, personally demonstrating a strong sense of accountability and responsibility at all levels of leadership.

7. Provide training and development opportunities to enhance employees' skills and capabilities. When employees feel equipped to handle their responsibilities, they are more likely to take accountability for their actions.

> *"Success on any major scale requires you to accept responsibility. In the final analysis, the one quality that all successful people have is the ability to take on responsibility."*
> Michael Korda

GROUP DISCUSSION QUESTIONS

1. What does accountability and responsibility mean to you in the context of your (a) work responsibilities, or (b) company promises or commitments?

2. Share an example of a time when you witnessed someone demonstrating a high level of accountability. What was the result?

3. What barriers would hinder improving accountability in our workplace? How could these challenges be overcome?

4. In what ways can accountability and responsibility impact our present work culture and market brand? What are the long-term benefits of embracing responsibility as a company core value?

5. What might be potential consequences of a lack of accountability/responsibility in our workplace environment?

6. What role would feedback play in fostering accountability? What are the dangers of a feedback system?

7. What practices or activities could be implemented to cultivate a greater sense company accountability?

8. How can leaders effectively model and promote accountability and responsibility within their teams and across the organization?

9. How could accountability and responsibility impact customer satisfaction and loyalty? Why?

10. How could our accountability be measured as a company brand?

> *"It is not only what we do, but also what we do not do,*
> *for which we are accountable."*
> Moliere

EXERCISE #1 – Accountability Case Studies

Divide the employees into small groups and provide each group with a set of accountability case studies. The case studies should depict real-life scenarios where the existence or lack of accountability or responsibility played a significant role in the outcome. In their groups, employees should discuss and analyze each case study, identifying the key elements of accountability and the impact it had on the situation. They can also brainstorm alternative approaches if accountability was lacking. Afterward, groups can present their findings and engage in a larger group discussion about the importance of accountability/responsibility and the lessons learned from the case studies.

EXERCISE #2 – Responsibility Simulation

Create a simulated work scenario where employees are assigned responsibilities within a team. The scenario should involve interdependent tasks and a common objective. Throughout the simulation, introduce challenges, changes, or obstacles that require individuals to demonstrate accountability and take responsibility for their assigned tasks. After the simulation, facilitate a debriefing session where employees reflect on their experiences, share insights, and discuss the impact of accountability or responsibility on teamwork, collaboration, and achieving the common objective. Encourage participants to discuss the challenges they faced and how being accountable or taking responsibility helped overcome them.

Note: You can design the scenarios to focus on either individual or corporate accountability.

EXERCISE #3 – Accountability Circle Reflection

Form small team circles consisting of three to five employees. In these circles, each employee takes turns sharing a recent work situation or project where they felt a strong sense of accountability or responsibility. They should describe the context, their role, and the actions they took to demonstrate accountability. The other members of the circle actively listen and ask clarifying questions to gain a deeper understanding of the situation. After each person shares, the group can provide feedback and insights, highlighting the positive impact of accountability and responsibility in each scenario. This exercise promotes peer learning, reflection, and the reinforcement of accountability/responsibility as a valuable core value.

Note: You can ask the employees to think of either individual or corporate accountability situations.

Remember to debrief and facilitate discussions after each exercise to ensure employees understand the lessons learned and can apply them to their work environment effectively.

"Responsibility equals accountability equals ownership. And a sense of ownership is the most powerful weapon a team or organization can have."
Pat Summitt

Chapter 9
Respect (Brand)

"Respect is the cornerstone of any successful organization. When individuals feel valued and appreciated, they become motivated and committed to achieving common goals."
Garry Ridge

GENERAL

The corporate core value of respect encompasses treating both employees and customers with dignity and consideration. It includes recognizing the inherent worth and unique contributions of every person, regardless of their position or relationship. Respect extends beyond mere politeness and is rooted in a culture of equality. Respect manifests itself in actively listening to others, valuing their opinions, and creating an atmosphere where all voices are heard and honored.

A respectful corporate culture encourages open and honest communication. It promotes trust, integrity, and ethical behavior, ensuring that both employees and customers feel safe and comfortable expressing their thoughts and concerns without fear of negative reactions or put-downs. For employees this core value recognizes work-life balance and fosters an environment that supports their personal well-being. For customers it often means patience and self-control in dealing with complaints.

Good leaders exhibit respect to both coworkers and customers. They treat others the way they would want to be treated. Respect means giving some form of deference to the needs, position, or abilities of others. Respect does not mean always agreeing with others ideas or feelings. It does, however recognize that others have the right to hold certain beliefs or concerns, just as you can hold beliefs that are different or even opposed to their positions.

By embracing the core value of respect, organizations cultivate a positive and inclusive work environment for employees. This leads to enhanced collaboration, increased employee satisfaction, improved decision-making, and ultimately to sustainable success and growth.

When customers are treated with respect, the expected result is customer loyalty and increased brand recognition.

BASIC ASPECTS OF RESPECT

Respect promotes equality by recognizing the diversity of individuals, including their backgrounds, experiences, perspectives, and identities. It involves creating an environment in which both employees and customers feel welcome and valued. Thus it upholds the principle of equality, treating everyone with fairness and impartiality. It ensures that the rights of others are not violated.

Respect requires open and transparent communication. It must include active listening, empathy, and understanding, fostering an atmosphere where individuals feel comfortable expressing their thoughts, ideas, or concerns.

Regularly expressing appreciation reinforces a culture of respect. Employees deserve recognition for their contributions. Customers should be valued and thanked for their concerns or suggestions.

Respect is rooted in consideration and esteem for others. It includes respecting the emotions, perspectives, and contributions of others, fostering an environment that appreciates the contributions of others.

One of the by-products of respect is trust. Respect builds trust among employees and clients. When individuals feel respected, they are more likely to trust their colleagues or associates, fostering stronger and more permanent relationships. Respect also encourages individuals to act with honesty, fairness, and accountability in their interactions.

Ethical conduct promotes a culture of respect and ensures that others are treated with dignity and fairness.

Respectful organizations prioritize constructive conflict resolution. Since open dialogue is encouraged, finding mutually beneficial solutions is often more easily achieved. Resolving conflicts respectfully helps maintain positive relationship, resulting in a harmonious work environment or company-client relationship.

By consistently reinforcing the significance of respect, organizations empower their employees to create a positive and inclusive work environment, enhancing employee morale, productivity, teamwork, and customer satisfaction. Respect sets the foundation for a thriving organizational culture that attracts and retains top talent. This core value then spills over to customer service and marketing strategies, resulting in a strong client following and a good company reputation.

> *"When respect is embedded in the DNA of a company, it becomes a guiding principle for decision-making and behavior at all levels."*
> Gail Kelly

ILLUSTRATION: Starbucks

In 2015, Starbucks, the global coffeehouse chain, faced a significant incident at one of its Philadelphia stores that became a catalyst for reevaluating and reinforcing its commitment to respect and inclusivity. Two African American customers visited the store and requested to use the restroom without making a purchase. The store manager denied their request, leading to a misunderstanding and ultimately involving of the police. The incident sparked outrage and raised allegations of racial profiling against Starbucks.

In response, Starbucks' CEO Kevin Johnson took immediate action. He personally apologized to the two customers involved and publicly expressed deep regret for the incident. Recognizing the need for systemic change, Johnson pledged to address the issue head-on and make Starbucks a beacon of inclusivity.

Starbucks closed all of its stores in the USA for an afternoon on May 29, 2018, for a company-wide racial bias training program. About 175,000 employees participated! It raised awareness and provided tools to address unconscious biases while promoting respect.

Starbucks' swift response and commitment in addressing the incident played a crucial role in rebuilding trust among its customers, employees, and the public. The company's proactive measures to confront racial bias demonstrated their dedication to creating an inclusive environment for everyone who enters their stores. By acknowledging the situation and taking responsibility, Starbucks not only rectified the situation but also emerged as a leader in promoting diversity and inclusivity within the corporate world.[1]

"Respect for people is the bedrock of any thriving business. It creates an environment where everyone feels heard, valued, and empowered to contribute their best."
Richard Branson

PRACTICAL TIPS

Treating others with respect is often fundamental in creating a positive workplace culture. Here are some easy tips to help implement respect within your organization:

1. Leaders should consistently model respectful behavior.

2. Create channels for customers or employees to express their thoughts and concerns in a respectful manner, no matter the nature of the communication.

3. Ensure that all employees and customers feel valued, regardless of their background, gender, ethnicity, or any other characteristic.

4. Clearly communicate that discrimination, harassment, or bullying will not be tolerated, either in the organization or with customers.

5. Implement programs that cover topics such as communication, cultural sensitivity, and conflict resolution.

6. Equip employees with the skills to address conflicts respectfully and find constructive solutions.

7. Create a clear and comprehensive Code of Conduct that outlines expected behaviors and the importance of respect toward both employees and customers.

8. Solicit feedback from employees and customers through surveys or feedback sessions.

"Treat your employees with respect, and they will go above and beyond to serve your customers and achieve exceptional results."
Mary Barra

GROUP DISCUSSION QUESTIONS

1. What does the company core value of respect mean to you personally? How does it relate to your work and interactions with other employees or customers?

2. What examples of respectful or disrespectful behaviors have you witnessed or experienced? How did those behaviors affect the work environment or customer relationships?

3. How does respect contribute to a positive workplace culture? What are some specific benefits that can result from such a culture?

4. In what ways can a lack of respect hinder productivity or sales for our organization? Can you share any personal experiences?

5. What role must leadership play in fostering a culture of respect? How can leaders actively demonstrate and promote respect?

6. How can the company improve its communications to enhance the core value of respect in your department or the company?

7. What strategies, techniques, or practices can be employed to ensure respectful communication between employees or with customers?

8. How can our organization measure and evaluate the level of respect within our workplace or in customer relationships?

9. What are some potential consequences of not prioritizing respect as a core value within our company? How might these consequences impact employees, customers, and the company?

10. How can employees hold others accountable for demonstrating respect in their daily interactions? What mechanisms or practices can be implemented to encourage and reinforce respectful behavior?

> *"Respect is a force that transforms organizations.*
> *It brings out the best in people, fuels collaboration,*
> *and drives sustainable success."*
> Tim Ryan

EXERCISE #1 – Empathy Building Exercise

1. Divide participants into small groups.

2. Provide each group with a scenario or case study that involves a challenging interpersonal situation in the workplace.

3. Instruct participants to discuss and empathize with each person involved in the scenario, considering their thoughts, feelings, and perspectives.

4. After the discussion, have participants share their insights with the larger group, highlighting how empathy and understanding contribute to a respectful work environment.

5. Facilitate a group reflection on the exercise, discussing the impact of empathy on communication, conflict resolution, and teamwork.

EXERCISE #2 – Respectful Communication Workshop

1. Conduct a workshop on developing respectful communication skills.

2. Begin with an overview of respectful communication principles, such as active listening, using inclusive language, and maintaining a positive tone.

3. Divide participants into small groups and provide them with communication scenarios that involve potential conflicts or misunderstandings.

4. Instruct participants to practice respectful communication techniques to navigate the scenarios effectively.

5. After the role-playing exercises, facilitate a group discussion to debrief the experience, allowing participants to share insights, challenges, and lessons learned.

6. Provide additional guidance and resources for improving communication skills and reinforcing the importance of respectful communication among coworkers and with customers.

EXERCISE #3 – Value Alignment Activity

1. Divide participants into small groups and provide each group with a set of cards that represent various core values, including respect.

2. Instruct the groups to discuss and rank the values in order of importance. They should focus on how respect should be prioritized.

3. After the ranking exercise, bring the groups together for a group discussion. Ask each group to present their rankings and reasoning.

4. Facilitate a discussion on the commonalities and differences in the rankings, highlighting the significance of respect as a core value and its impact on organizational culture and success.

5. Encourage participants to reflect on ways they can personally embody and promote respect in their daily interactions.

BONUS IDEAS
1. Establish a "Respect Committee."
2. Create a "Respectful Workplace Policy" or "Code of Respect Policy."
3. Implement a mentorship or coaching program.
4. Incorporate promoting respect into hiring procedures and training.
5. Recognize and celebrate respectful behaviors.

Remember to debrief and facilitate discussions after each exercise to ensure employees understand the lessons learned and can apply them to their work environment effectively.

"Respect is the foundation of trust.
Without trust, collaboration falters,
and progress stagnates."
John Mackey

Chapter 10
Social Responsibility

"The business of business should not just be about money, it should be about responsibility. It should be about public good, not private greed."
Anita Roddick

GENERAL

A company core value of social responsibility refers to a commitment to conducting business in a manner that takes into account the well-being of society, the local community, and the environment. It goes beyond the pursuit of profit as the sole focus of the organization. It emphasizes the ethical obligations a company has toward the communities in which it operates and society in general. Profit is important but it is not necessarily the ultimate objective. A non-financial mission may be the driving force of the organization.

A broad definition of social responsibility involves a company addressing the impact of their actions on employees, customers, suppliers, local communities, and the environment. It involves making conscious decisions and taking actions that align with principles of sustainability, ethical conduct, positive social impact, and minimal negative impact on the environment.

Companies that prioritize social responsibility integrate it into their entire business operations. They want to minimize any negative impact associated with their activities while maximizing the positive contributions of the company. This can manifest itself in various forms, such as implementing fair labor practices, supporting community development initiatives, reducing the carbon footprint, promoting diversity, or engaging in various philanthropic endeavors.

A core value of social responsibility extends beyond just legal compliance. It seeks to proactively address broader business and societal challenges. It generally includes a proactive approach in order to be a force for positive change. By incorporating social responsibility as a core value, businesses acknowledge that their long-term viability is connected to the well-being of the communities and environment in which they operate.

"If you want to achieve greatness,
stop asking for permission.
Start giving back."
Unknown

CHARACTERISTICS AND ASPECTS

Social responsibility desires to make a positive impact on society and often recognizes the importance of preserving the environment. It may include trying to minimize its ecological footprint, reduce pollution, and support conservation efforts.

Socially responsible companies often engage with local communities and contribute to their well-being. This may involve supporting local charities, special projects, or other local social causes. Such activity may not be limited to the location of the corporate headquarters.

Some companies committed to social responsibility may require their supply chains to adhere to certain ethical or social practices. This may include fair treatment of workers or promoting sustainable business practices. This can be the most difficult aspect of this core value because companies must rely on the commitment of their suppliers.

Socially responsible companies generally prioritize the personal growth of their employees. They provide a safe work environment, pay fair compensation, and encourage work-life balance. Many companies do these things, but socially conscious companies are primarily focused on the well-being of people or places.

Socially responsible companies prioritize legal accountability and uphold regulatory compliance throughout their organization. Short-term success is certainly desired but this core value is directed more at long-lasting sustainability. Therefore, conforming to laws and regulations is a priority.

Companies that significantly prioritize social responsibility can differentiate themselves from competitors and potentially gain a competitive edge in the marketplace. Employees are typically more engaged and proud to work for organizations that actively contribute to a better society.

In summary, social responsibility in the business context is not just a moral obligation but a strategic imperative. By integrating social responsibility into core values, companies try to enhance their reputation, build trust, and foster long-term success. In the process they positively impact the communities in which they operate.

> *"Success is not just about making money.*
> *It's about making a difference."*
> Unknown

ILLUSTRATION: Patagonia

One notable business success story that exemplifies this core value is the case of Patagonia, an outdoor clothing and gear company. They have demonstrated strong commitments to the environment and to social responsibility. This has not only earned them a positive reputation but has also contributed to their business success.

Patagonia promotes using sustainable materials, reducing waste, and being an advocate for recycling. They were among the first companies to produce fleece made from recycled plastic bottles and have since expanded their use of recycled materials across their product lines. By seeking sustainable alternatives they reduced their environmental impact and pleased environmentally conscious consumers.

Another example of their social strategy is their "Worn Wear" program. Patagonia encourages customers to repair and reuse their products by offering free repairs and refurbishment services. This not only extends the lifespan of their products but also promotes a culture of conscious consumption and discourages excessive waste.

Patagonia has launched campaigns addressing issues such as climate change, public lands preservation, and fair labor practices. For example, in 2017, the company donated all proceeds from their Black Friday sales, amounting to $10 million, to grassroots environmental organizations. This bold move not only showcased their commitment to the environment but also resonated with consumers who appreciated their genuine dedication to making a positive impact.

Despite encouraging customers to consume less and repair rather than replace, Patagonia has experienced consistent revenue growth. Their dedication to social responsibility has not hindered reasonable growth in profitability. Their strong brand reputation as a socially responsible company has built a loyal customer base.

The case of Patagonia highlights how embracing social responsibility as a core value can contribute to business success. By prioritizing sustainability, promoting conscious consumption, and engaging with social causes, Patagonia has not only attracted like-minded customers but has also inspired other companies to follow suit.[J1]

Negative examples

Volkswagen: The German carmaker admitted in 2015 that it had installed software in millions of diesel vehicles to cheat on emissions tests and make them appear more environmentally friendly than they were. The scandal cost the company billions of dollars in fines, lawsuits, recalls, and lost sales. Their reputation and trust among customers, regulators, and investors was extensively damaged.[J2]

BP Oil: This British oil giant was responsible for the largest offshore oil spill in U.S. history in 2010, when an explosion at its Deepwater Horizon rig in the Gulf of Mexico killed 11 workers and released millions of barrels of oil into the ocean. The spill caused widespread environmental and economic damage to the region, as well as health problems for the workers and residents. BP faced criminal charges, civil lawsuits, and public outrage for its negligence and poor handling of the crisis.[J3]

Wells Fargo: This American bank was exposed in 2016 for creating millions of fake accounts for customers without their consent or knowledge, in order to meet sales targets and earn bonuses. The fraudulent scheme harmed the customers' credit scores and finances, and violated their privacy and trust. Wells Fargo experienced regulatory fines, legal actions, customer defections, and a loss of reputation and credibility.[J4]

PRACTICAL TIPS

1. Form different teams to work together on projects that address social and environmental challenges.

2. Encourage employees to submit suggestions on how to implement innovative ideas that support social responsibility.

3. Provide resources and special training on social responsibility.

4. Implement strategic partnerships with external organizations that have similar social responsibility goals.

5. Use internal newsletters, company communication channels, and social media to communicate success stories.

6. Recognize and reward employees who actively contribute to social responsibility initiatives.

GROUP DISCUSSION QUESTIONS

1. What does social responsibility mean to you? Do you think it is important for businesses to embrace this subject as a core value? Why? Why not?

2. How do you think a company's commitment to social responsibility can positively impact its relationships with customers, employees, or the local community?

3. Can you think of any examples where a company faced significant backlash or damage due to a lack of social responsibility?

4. Do you think social responsibility initiatives contribute to a company's long-term financial success or do they just cost money?

5. How can social responsibility help attract top talent? Do you think employees are seeking to work for socially responsible organizations? Why? Why not?

6. What potential challenges or barriers would our company face in trying to implement or increase its social responsibility? How could these challenges be overcome?

7. Can you identify any departments or divisions in our company in which social responsibility is particularly crucial? Why do you think these areas require heightened attention to social responsibility?

8. What are some of the key social or environmental issues facing our company today? How can we address these issues?

9. Do you think social responsibility can foster innovation? Explain.

10. How can we strike a balance between our responsibility to shareholders for financial results and our responsibility to society?

11. How could our company collaborate with external organizations in our community to maximize our combined impact on society?

12. What specific actions could our company undertake to enhance our commitment to social responsibility?

EXERCISE #1 – Case Study Analysis

Divide employees into small groups and provide each group with a case study that highlights a real-world example of a company that has demonstrated a strong commitment to social responsibility. The case study could include information about the company's social initiatives, impact on communities, and positive outcomes. Instruct each group to analyze the case study, discuss the reasons behind the company's success, and identify key lessons and takeaways. Afterward, facilitate a group discussion in which each group shares their findings and insights. Encourage participants to discuss how the case study exemplifies the importance and benefits of social responsibility.

EXERCISE #2 – Ethical Dilemma Role-Play

Create small groups of employees and assign each group a different ethical dilemma related to social responsibility. These dilemmas could involve scenarios such as environmental conservation, fair labor practices, or community engagement. Instruct each group to role-play a scenario in which they explore the dilemma, discuss the various perspectives involved, and propose potential solutions that align with social responsibility principles. After each role-play, facilitate a group discussion where participants share their experiences, challenges encountered, and insights gained. Encourage reflection on the decision-making process and the impact of their proposed solutions on all stakeholders.

EXERCISE #3 – Interactive Workshop

Organize an interactive workshop in which employees actively participate in hands-on activities related to social responsibility. For example, you could set up stations or workshops on topics such as sustainability, community service, or ethical sourcing. Participants can engage in practical exercises like creating a sustainability plan for the workplace, organizing a volunteer project, or examining supply chain practices. Allow participants to collaborate, share ideas, and discuss the impact of their actions on society and the company. Encourage reflection on the workshop activities and facilitate a group discussion to connect their experiences to the importance of social responsibility as a core value.

Remember to debrief and facilitate discussions after each exercise to ensure employees understand the lessons learned and can apply them to their work environment effectively.

"A good company offers excellent products and services. A great company also offers excellent products and services but also strives to make the world a better place."
Philip Kotler

95

Chapter 11
Diversity

*"Diversity is not about how
we differ. It is about embracing
one another's uniqueness."*
Ola Joseph

GENERAL

The core value of diversity refers to recognizing that a workforce, composed of individuals from various backgrounds, experiences, cultures, and identities, is important for the success and growth of the organization. It involves an environment in which all employees are provided equal opportunities to contribute. Diversity, in an ideal environment, will not only apply to visible characteristics such as race, gender, and age but to diversity of thought, beliefs, and experience.

This core value is about creating an inclusive workplace culture in which individuals feel a sense of belonging, regardless of their differences. It includes actively seeking and embracing equality in the organization, including hiring practices, promotions, and decision-making. It goes beyond mere numbers and aims to provide an environment that encourages collaboration and respect for everyone.

An organization that values diversity recognizes that equality is not only ethically right but that it can be instrumental in driving ultimate company success. It acknowledges that diverse teams bring a wider range of insights, experiences, and ideas, which can lead to better decision-making. By including diversity as a core value, companies strive to cultivate a work environment that attracts top talent in order to better serve diverse customer bases. This commitment often requires implementing inclusive policies within the company structure that provide a safe space for employees to express themselves without fear of discrimination or bias.

"Diversity is being invited to the party;
inclusion is being asked to dance."
Verna Myers

ASPECTS AND CHARACTERISTICS

In order for this core value to be effective the company must ensure a diverse representation across all levels of the organization, including leadership positions. The initial objective should be to provide opportunities and career advancement for all employees, regardless of their background or personal identity.

The longer term goal is to foster an inclusive work environment where individuals feel valued and respected. The hope is that all employees contribute fully to the organization's success. This means that the company will try to create a workplace free from discrimination or prejudice based on factors such as race, gender, age, sexual orientation, disability, or any other diverse characteristic.

Embracing the power of diverse perspectives can help create innovation and creativity. This can contribute to developing new solutions to old problems within the organization. Management will encourage collaboration and teamwork across diverse teams, leveraging different backgrounds and perspectives in order to achieve better business decisions.

Communication is a key component of any business but can be particularly critical in companies with diverse populations. It requires promoting cultural competence among employees in order to enhance understanding and respect across diverse cultural norms. Words and actions can have different meanings in different cultures, therefore, training employees in just the minimum of different cultural nuances can produce a significant improvement in communication.

It can be helpful to engage employees in initiatives related to diversity and inclusion, seeking their input and feedback in order to stimulate opportunities for their active participation. Providing diversity training programs and resources that promote understanding will be necessary for building an inclusive workplace.

The company must also decide how involved they want to be in requiring diversity in their supply chain. Engaging in supplier diversity initiatives can be challenging. It is often much easier to partner with businesses owned by individuals from underrepresented groups than to require existing mature organizations to implement your requirements, particularly if your requirements cause significant changes in their organizations.

Establishing measurable goals to track progress is a desirable goal but much easier said than done. Measuring the actual impact on the bottom line of any productivity diversity statistics is not particularly easy. It is much easier to identify gaps in the make-up of the workforce and measure the absolute fall or growth in the underrepresented groups, than to measure the impact on the company bottom line.

Embracing diversity will be important for building strong relationships with diverse customer bases. Customers appreciate and connect with companies that speak with understanding about their unique needs. This can create increased customer loyalty and market share. Diversity often signals that the organization values fairness and equality.

Organizations that embrace diversity are often better equipped to navigate global markets because they understand diverse customer needs and adapt their products to different cultural contexts.

In summary, diversity and inclusion can foster a culture of innovation and creativity by bringing together diverse perspectives, experiences, and ideas. It can drive fresh thinking and will frequently challenge the status quo. It is possible by creating an inclusive environment companies can tap into a broader talent pool from diverse backgrounds and benefit from their unique skills and perspectives.

"Diversity is the art of
thinking independently together."
Malcolm Forbes

ILLUSTRATIONS

Microsoft Corporation

One notable business success story that exemplifies the importance of core values related to diversity is the case of Microsoft Corporation. Under the leadership of CEO Satya Nadella, Microsoft has made significant strides in fostering a diverse and inclusive workplace culture. This effort has positively impacted the company's performance and reputation.

Before Nadella took the helm in 2014, Microsoft faced criticism for its lack of diversity and inclusion in its workforce. Recognizing the need for change, Nadella implemented various initiatives that prioritized diversity as a core value within the company.

One key initiative was the establishment of diversity goals and targets. Microsoft publicly set targets to increase the representation of women and underrepresented minorities in its workforce and leadership positions. They implemented strategies focused on expanding the candidate pool to include diverse talent.

Microsoft prioritized creating an inclusive culture where employees could thrive. The company launched programs and employee resource groups (ERGs) to support diverse communities within the organization. These groups included Blacks, Asians, and LGBTQ+ groups. These ERGs provided a platform for employees to network, share experiences, and contribute to Microsoft's overall diversity and inclusion efforts.

By 2020, the company achieved gender pay equity and made significant progress in increasing the representation of women and underrepresented minorities in its workforce. Studies have shown that diverse teams at Microsoft have higher employee satisfaction, increased innovation, and better decision-making. The company has been recognized by various organizations for its initiatives, including being named as one of the top companies for diversity and inclusion by Diversity Inc.[K1]

Blick Shared Studios

Blick Shared Studios is an example of a small company's success. Blick, based in Dublin, Ireland, provides small art and design co-working space. The company recognized the value of diversity in the creative industry and made it a core principle of their business.

Blick actively sought to create an inclusive and diverse community within their co-working spaces. They established an environment that welcomed artists and designers from various backgrounds and cultures. They actively engaged with underrepresented communities and collaborated with organizations supporting marginalized groups to ensure a diverse range of members.

By embracing diversity, Blick experienced several positive outcomes. First, their diverse community attracted a broader range of creative talents, which enriched the overall artistic environment and sparked innovative collaborations. The variety of perspectives contributed to a more vibrant and dynamic atmosphere within their spaces.

Second, their commitment to inclusion created a supportive and welcoming environment for all members. This inclusivity fostered a sense of belonging and encouraged participants to express their creativity freely and collaborate with others. This led to enhanced productivity and output. Furthermore, Blick actively organized events that celebrated diverse artists and cultural expressions. This allowed members to connect and gain exposure to different artistic practices and perspectives.

Ultimately, Blick's commitment to diversity and inclusion contributed to their business success. Their example shows that even smaller companies can benefit significantly from embracing diversity and inclusion as core values, leading to positive business outcomes and a stronger sense of community.[K2]

"Diversity is a fact, but inclusion
is a choice we make every day. As leaders,
we have to put out the message that we
embrace and not just tolerate diversity."
Nellie Borrero

PRACTICAL TIPS

1. Set specific goals for workforce representation and leadership diversity.

2. Create platforms or channels for employees to share their thoughts and ideas related to company initiatives.

3. Conduct audits to identify opportunities for improvement.

4. Offer or require cross-cultural training programs.

5. Ensure that interview panels and selection committees include diverse representation.

6. Talk about success stories publicly.

7. Partner with other organizations that focus on diversity.

8. Include diversity as a component in performance evaluations and in the feedback process. Ask leaders to describe their diversity initiates during their performance evaluations.

9. Collaborate with a minority owned company that would help both companies improve their business and increase racial understanding and harmony.

GROUP DISCUSSION QUESTIONS

1. What does diversity and inclusion mean to you personally and how do you see it impacting our organization?

2. Can you share an experience where you felt included or valued in a diverse team? How did it impact the team's success?

3. How can diversity drive innovation and creativity within our company? Can you provide examples?

4a. What are some potential challenges or barriers that our company may face trying to create a diverse and inclusive work environment?

4b. What strategies could be implemented to address any biases or barriers that may exist within our organization?

5. How can unconscious biases hinder diversity and inclusion efforts?

6. What role can leadership play in fostering a culture of diversity and inclusion within our organization? Provide examples.

7. Do you think diversity and inclusion initiatives align with our company's overall mission and values? Why? Why not?

8. What strategies could the company implement to promote the recruitment and retention of diverse talent within our organization?

9. How can we ensure that diverse voices are heard and valued in meetings or decision-making processes in our organization?

10. In your opinion what steps do we need to take immediately to create a safe and inclusive work environment where employees feel comfortable expressing their thoughts and opinions? Explain.

> *"Diversity and inclusion, which are the real grounds*
> *for creativity, must remain at the center of what we do."*
> Marco Bizzarri

EXERCISE #1 – Privilege Walk

The privilege walk exercise helps individuals understand their privileges and the impact of privilege on opportunities and experiences. In this exercise:

1. Create a line on the floor or use tape to mark a starting point and an endpoint.
2. Ask a series of questions that prompt participants to take a step forward or backward based on their experiences of privilege or disadvantage.
3. Either after each question or at the end of all questions, facilitate a discussion to reflect on the exercise and the disparities that arise due to different levels of privilege.
4. Encourage participants to share their thoughts and emotions throughout the exercise, fostering empathy and understanding.

EXERCISE #2 – Diversity in Perspective

1. Divide participants into small groups and assign each group a specific topic or scenario to discuss. If you do not have particular subjects you want to use, choose one of the questions from the Group Discussion Questions above.
2. Instruct each group to approach the topic from a particular perspective (e.g., cultural, generational, or gender-based).
3. After the discussions, reconvene as a larger group and have each small group share their perspectives.
4. Facilitate a debriefing session to discuss the different viewpoints and the value of diverse perspectives in decision-making and problem-solving.

EXERCISE #3 – Diversity Circles

Diversity circles provide an opportunity for individuals to share personal experiences related to diversity and inclusion.

1. Form small groups of 4-6 participants and provide each group with a set of diverse identity cards (e.g., race, gender, sexual orientation, age, ability, religion).
2. Instruct each participant to select one identity card that they feel most connected to or have experience with.
3. Ask participants to share personal stories, challenges, or achievements related to their chosen identity card.
4. Encourage active listening, respect, and empathy in groups.
5. After the sharing session, invite participants to reflect on the exercise and discuss how understanding diverse experiences can contribute to a more supportive workplace environment.

Remember to debrief and facilitate discussions after each exercise to ensure employees understand the lessons learned and can apply them to their work environment effectively.

> *"Diversity is the one true thing we all*
> *have in common. Celebrate it every day."*
> Author Unknown

Chapter 12
Fun

*"Fun is one of the most important
and underrated ingredients in
any successful venture."*
Richard Branson

GENERAL

The core value of fun generally means that an organization wants to create an enjoyable, lighthearted, and engaging workplace environment. It involves encouraging a sense of enthusiasm, playfulness, and joy in the physical workplace. It often recognizes the importance of work-life balance and employee well-being. Fun as a core value means infusing elements of enjoyment and excitement into the work environment, making it a place where employees genuinely look forward to coming each day.

It does not mean that financial results or customer satisfaction are not highly valued! Rather it is a strategy to produce an atmosphere that promotes creativity, innovation, collaboration, and a highly positive culture, in order to achieve business success.

Organizations that prioritize fun don't believe that work must be a mundane and serious affair. They actively encourage employees to inject humor, levity, and a playful spirit into their daily activities. This can occur by organizing team-building activities, celebrating milestones and achievements, hosting social events, or incorporating gamification into work processes.

When fun is a core value, employees are encouraged to express their creativity and think outside the box. This may involve implementing innovative ideas, experimenting with new approaches, or finding unconventional solutions to problems. Such an environment desires to cultivate a positive attitude toward learning and risk-taking.

This core value would not be appropriate for all organizations and is usually implemented where creativity, fun, or entertainment is an inherent part of the products or services of the organization. Therefore it might be a core value of a toy company, digital game company, or a sports and entertainment company. It is most used where creativity is an important component of company success.

Fun as a core value promotes a positive and vibrant workplace culture that encourages positive employee well-being. By prioritizing fun, organizations create an atmosphere in which employees thrive, leading to increased productivity and higher job satisfaction.

> *"The success of a company is determined by*
> *the atmosphere it creates. If people are smiling,*
> *having fun, and enjoying their work,*
> *that's when the magic happens."*
> Tony Hsieh

CHARACTERISTICS AND ASPECTS

Embracing fun encourages a positive approach to work and promotes a sense of enjoyment, relaxation, and humor in the workplace. It involves infusing elements of fun and levity into daily activities and interactions in order to produce short periods when the employee is not thinking about work.

A fun-oriented business core value desires to promote optimism and enthusiasm. It provides a supportive environment that encourages teamwork, creativity, and mutual respect. It can also involve providing an alternative physical location to work where the atmosphere is not four walls surrounding a desk.

Fun as a core value is often intended to stimulate creativity and innovation by encouraging employees to explore new ideas and take calculated risks. Wild and crazy ideas are often encouraged. It seeks to create an environment where individuals feel inspired to contribute new ideas and opinions. They are encouraged to participate in the work rather than simply follow a set routine of work instructions. A game company would encourage employees to play the games and a toy company would give toys to the employees to play with or take home to their families.

A fun core value might also be used by employers who wish to promote work-life balance. The importance of personal well-being may be the primary core value of such employers. Practices and policies that enable employees to maintain a healthy equilibrium between their work responsibilities and personal lives can lead to increased job satisfaction happy employees. Fun activities promote physical and mental health. Flexible working arrangements and stress management techniques are often encouraged.

These characteristics contribute to an organizational culture that produces enjoyment, fulfillment, and a sense of shared purpose.

"Fun is the secret ingredient that keeps teams engaged and motivated.
It's what turns an ordinary workplace into an extraordinary one."
Stephen Richards

ILLUSTRATION: Zappos

One business success story that exemplifies the importance of fun as a core value is that of Zappos, an online shoe and clothing retailer known for its exceptional customer service. Zappos was founded in 1999 and gained prominence under the leadership of Tony Hsieh. Hsieh recognized the significance of creating a fun and engaging work environment as a means to drive employee satisfaction, customer loyalty, and ultimately business success.

Zappos infused fun as a core value into its culture by introducing a unique coming-on-board program called "Zappos Culture Camp," where new hires spend their first week learning about the company's values, including the importance of having fun. The program includes interactive games, team-building activities, and opportunities to socialize with colleagues.

The company also encourages self-expression and creativity among its employees. They have an annual "Zapponian Idol" talent show where employees showcase their talents and entertain their peers. They celebrate holidays and special occasions with themed parties, costume contests, and office decorations. These activities create a sense of camaraderie, foster strong relationships, and boost morale.

Additionally, Zappos incorporates fun into its customer service approach. Their representatives are empowered to engage with customers in a lighthearted and personalized manner, often going above and beyond to deliver exceptional experiences. For instance, they have been known to send surprise gifts or engage in impromptu acts of kindness to delight customers.

The emphasis on fun at Zappos has yielded remarkable results. The company has achieved significant growth and financial success. They have received numerous accolades for their outstanding workplace culture, including being named one of Fortune's "100 Best Companies to Work For" multiple times.

The impact of this core value is evident in Zappos' high employee retention rates and strong customer loyalty. Employees feel a strong sense of belonging and enjoy their work, leading to increased job satisfaction and commitment. Customers appreciate the personalized and enjoyable experiences, leading to repeat business and positive word-of-mouth sales.

The success of Zappos is an example of incorporating fun as a core value. By creating an environment that values enjoyment, creativity, and positive relationships, the company has achieved business success and built a strong and passionate community of employees and customers.[L]

"Incorporating fun into the workplace isn't just about having a good time; it's about fostering a culture that promotes creativity, collaboration, and innovation."
Arianna Huffington

PRACTICAL TIPS

1. Fun Committee: Establish a committee or a group of employees responsible for planning and organizing fun activities.

2. Fun Fridays: Designate a specific day of the week or month, such as "Fun Fridays," where employees engage in activities that promote fun.

3. Office Decorations: Encourage employees to decorate their workspaces in a fun and personalized way.

4. Break Areas: Set up designated areas in the office for employees to unwind and have fun during breaks.

5. Fun Contests: Organize regular fun challenges or contests that engage employees and create a sense of friendly competition.

6. Rewards: Surprise employees with small treats, snacks, or rewards.

7. Communications: Create a newsletter or communication channel where employees can share funny stories.

8. Charity: Organize volunteer or charity events where employees can come together to contribute to a cause.

9. Lunch: Host lunch and learning sessions where employees can enjoy engaging presentations or interactive discussions.

10. Holidays: Celebrate holidays that align with the company's values or industry. You can even make up a new one just for your employees.

The key is to have an inclusive and enjoyable work environment that allows employees to find joy in their daily work experiences. But there is always an eye on the success of the organization.

"Fun is the fuel that drives passion and motivation.
It keeps people excited about what they do and
inspires them to achieve greatness."
Mark Zuckerberg

GROUP DISCUSSION QUESTIONS

1. What does "fun" mean to you in the context of your workplace environment?

2. How could incorporating fun as a core value impact employee morale and job satisfaction? Why?

3. Can you recall a time when a fun activity or event at work positively influenced your productivity or engagement? Explain.

4. What role do you think fun plays in fostering creativity and innovation within an organization? Why?

5. Do you think a fun work environment affects the way employees approach challenges and problem-solving? Can you give examples?

6. Can you think of any potential concerns or challenges that may arise if fun is a core value? How might those challenges be overcome?

7. Do you think fun, as a core value of our organization, can have an impact on overall customer satisfaction? Why?

8. Do you think fun activities or initiatives in the workplace can help alleviate stress and prevent burnout among employees? Explain.

9. How might the perception of professionalism be affected if fun is emphasized as a core value? Is that good or bad for our company?

10. How would fun, as a core value, contribute to the overall reputation and image of our organization?

EXERCISE #1 – Fun Values Brainstorming Session

1. Divide the employees into small groups.

2. Provide each group with a list of core values (including fun) and a large sheet of paper or a whiteboard.

3. Instruct each group to brainstorm and discuss examples of how the core value of fun can positively impact the workplace and contribute to the organization's success.

4. Encourage employees to think creatively and come up with specific ideas and scenarios.

5. After a designated time, ask each group to present their ideas to the whole group and facilitate a discussion around the importance of fun as a core value.

EXERCISE #2 – Fun Team Challenge

1. Divide the employees into teams.

2. Assign each team a fun challenge that requires collaboration, problem-solving, and creativity.

3. The challenge could involve building a structure using limited materials, solving a puzzle, designing a fun game or activity for the workplace, or designing a game center in the workplace.

4. Provide a set time limit for the teams to complete the challenge.

5. After the challenge, debrief the activity and discuss how the elements of fun, teamwork, and creativity contributed to the success of each team.

6. Facilitate a discussion on how these elements can be applied to the workplace and the importance of fun as a core value in fostering a positive and productive work environment.

ALTERNATIVELY: Do this activity at different times with different employee groups, making sure the activity is substantial. In one session allow the groups no break in the process above. In other groups stop the process at some point and do some fun actively for 10-15 minutes. Observe if the output (quantity and quality) of one group is better than another.

EXERCISE #3 – Fun Activity Reflection

1. Start the session by engaging the employees in a fun activity, such as a team game, trivia, or icebreaker.

2. After the activity, gather the employees in a circle and ask each person to share how they felt during the activity and what they enjoyed about it.

3. Facilitate a discussion on the positive impact of fun activities in creating a sense of camaraderie, boosting morale, and fostering a positive work environment.

4. Connect the above comments and discussions to the corporate core value of fun, highlighting how incorporating fun into the workplace can have positive effects on employee engagement, productivity, and overall well-being.

5. Encourage employees to share their own ideas for incorporating more enjoyment into the workplace and discuss potential barriers or challenges that might need to be overcome.

Remember to debrief and facilitate discussions after each exercise to ensure employees understand the lessons learned and can apply them to their work environment effectively.

"When you infuse fun into the workplace, you create a positive cycle where happy employees lead to satisfied customers, which in turn leads to business success."
Tony Hsieh

Appendix A – Implementation

First allow us to repeat some information previously outlined in the "Introduction" of this book.

Implementation Principle:
We believe that in implementing a business core value strategy it is necessary to develop that core value in the individual employees. If the desired core value is not instilled in the employees to some degree, there will be little hope that an effective strategy can be implemented for the company.

Purpose of Company Core Values:
Following are the common ten reasons that an employer would establish and implement core values in their organization:

1. Improved decision-making
2. Positive company culture
3. Increased employee engagement
4. Ethical business conduct
5. Customer loyalty
6. Competitive advantage
7. Strategic alignment of policies and strategies
8. Dynamic innovation
9. Effective leadership
10. Outstanding business reputation

A company might generally have all of these objectives but several would likely be the most important and be the primary reason for implementing core values within the organization.

CHOOSE Core Values book:
Our *Powerful Business Strategies* book (this book) is basically a training guide or resource for the employer. It is intended to be used in conjunction with another book, *CHOOSE Core Values,* that is a resource for the individual employee. The *CHOOSE* book is in our Life Planning Series and can be obtained at:
https://www.amazon.com/dp/195235949X

Employer Implementation:

1. Planning, Goals, and Objectives

Your intended plans or strategies for implementing core values in your company should be consistent with your Company Plan (mission, vision, goals, marketing strategies, action plans, etc.). If you do not have a formal plan your intentions should be consistent with whatever strategies you are following to create or maintain a successful business venture. If you do not have a formal plan or any real marketing strategies our suggestion would be that you develop at least the key components of a plan before you proceed to develop core values in your business environment. The important objective here is to know that what you are going to do in the area of core values is consistent with your business concept.

2. Company Policies, Standards, Codes, etc.

In addition to Standard Operating Procedures and Codes of Conduct, successful businesses often develop a large range of formal documents to ensure clarity, consistency, and compliance to company or legal requirements. The existence of any formal documents is a function of the size and maturity of the company. Industry standards would also have some influence on whether any of these documents exist in your company. Here is a listing of other types of formal documents that a successful business might have:

a. Employee Handbook: A comprehensive guide that provides employees with information about company policies, procedures, benefits, and expectations. It serves as a reference for both new and existing employees.

b. Mission, Vision, and Values Statements: Documents that articulate the company's overall mission, vision for the future and its core values. These statements provide a guiding framework for decision-making and goal-setting.

c. Strategic Plan: A document outlining the organization's goals, strategies, and action plans. It provides a roadmap for achieving the company's long-term vision and mission.

d. Marketing Plan: A comprehensive document that outlines the company's business model, goals, target market, competition analysis, and financial projections. It serves as a roadmap for the business's <u>short-term</u> development and growth.

e. Job Descriptions: Documents detailing the roles, responsibilities, qualifications, and expectations for each position in the organization.

f. Performance Appraisal Forms: Documents outlining the criteria and process for evaluating employee performance. This includes forms used during performance reviews.

g. Training Manuals: Manuals that provide detailed information on job responsibilities, processes, and procedures.

h. Succession Plans: Documents outlining strategies for identifying and developing talent within the organization.

i. Communication Plan: A plan outlining the strategies, channels, restrictions, responsibility, and frequency of communication both internally and externally.

j. Crisis Management Plan: A document that outlines procedures and responsibilities in the event of a crisis or emergency. It includes communication strategies, resource allocation, and steps for recovery.

k. Financial Policies and Procedures: Documents detailing financial management policies, budgeting procedures, and financial reporting requirements and standards.

l. Customer Service Standards: Documents outlining the company's commitment to providing high-quality customer service. It may include service agreements and guidelines for customer interactions.

m. Data Protection and Privacy Policies: Documents outlining how the company collects, processes, and protects sensitive information, ensuring compliance with data protection laws.

n. Quality Assurance and Control Documents: Documents outlining processes and procedures to ensure the quality of products or services. This may include quality control checklists, inspection procedures, audit procedures, and testing protocols.

Again, the process of developing or implementing core values in the organization should be consistent with existing company policies and perspectives. Establishing core values may require that some of these documents be modified.

3. Resource Allocation

Don't forget that everything costs money. If you are implementing anything new or adding to existing functions within the company there will be some cost. Make sure you have the funding before you start planning and implementing new or improved functions in the organization. Typically there will be a cost for:

     a. communications
     b. training and development
        • resources, materials, and facilities if necessary
        • training staff or third-party training fees
        • employee down-time
     c. collecting performance data
     d. obtaining customer feedback
     e. rewards, recognition and celebrations

4. Communication (Company)

     a. Channels (Announcements, Newsletters, Bulletin Boards)
     b. Content development or acquisition

5. Leadership

It will be necessary to have executives, managers, and supervisors fully on board and trained to support and promote the core values that are to be implemented. Before any general communication is made to the press or employees about new core value initiatives or plans, the role of leaders should be defined and communicated. Leaders should be trained first and be prepared for whatever role they will be required to play in the implementation of the new core value strategy.

6. Training Programs

The amount, complexity, and cost of training programs will depend on what new plans and strategies are to be implemented. Generally it will be necessary to develop training plans for some or all of the following:

     a. Communication skills
     b. Interpersonal skills
     c. Character attributes
     d. Ability skills
     e. Coaching and mentoring
     f. Leadership qualities

In addition, it is often wise to have resources available for employees who want to develop skills on their own time. Be prepared to provide access to books and other resources that can be loaned or purchased by the employee. Provide a list of free or inexpensive online courses, webinars, conferences, etc.

7. Performance Measurement

If you are serious about core values having significant impact on the organization, you will want to know if you are being successful in your efforts. Measurements would not be necessary initially but depending on how quickly and how much you attempt to implement, knowing the impact will begin to be very important when the full strategy has been put in place. If you are spending substantial sums, you need to know that you are achieving your objectives.

8. Recognition, Rewards, and Celebration

Your implementation plans should include these three functions. They should not be ignored if you are seriously trying to change your company culture. There will be a time and cost for these motivational aspects of your program.

9. Other Strategies

In addition to the strategies and functions discussed above there are other activities that could be implemented to help promote or implement the chosen core values.

    a. Contests

    b. Work assignments: (1) cross department training, collaboration, teamwork, (2) special projects, or (3) increased responsibility.

    c. Job descriptions and performance reviews

    d. Orientation promotion and training

    e. Customer feedback

    f. *CHOOSE Core Values* book
- Give to all employees upon hiring
- Give to all employees after 3 months
- Give to employee when attend first training program

USE OF DISCUSSION QUESTIONS

There are discussion questions both in this book and in the *CHOOSE Core Values* book. If part of your training and implementation program is to have small group discussions or large meetings in which these questions are discussed, it will be necessary to combine and integrate the discussion questions from both books to achieve the type of focus you want for your group discussions.

You might want to develop discussion questions specifically for your team leaders or management. You might have other discussion questions for larger audiences. These discussion questions could also be separated between those directed at the personal employee and those focused on the company.

USE OF GROUP EXERCISES

There are three Group Exercises described at the end of each chapter. These could be used by group leaders at the team level or they could be used for larger meetings where the audience would be split into smaller groups for the purpose of the exercise. These exercises could be run by one of the members in the HR Department or a third-party hired for that purpose.

The team exercises could be directed by team leaders at convenient times or scheduled for Friday afternoons when business might be less hectic or when employees tend to be less busy or productive.

SPECIAL PERMISSION TO USE:
If any employer purchases this book, the author and Extra-mile Publishing grant that employer the right to copy and use information from this book or any of the books in the Life Planning Series if such information or copies are used solely for the internal training of company employees.

Appendix B – Leadership

"Real leadership...comes from realizing
that the time has come to move
beyond waiting to doing."
Madeleine Albright

NOTES

#1 Leadership can be both a core value of a business or a business technique or process to implement other core values. It depends on how leadership or core values are conceptualized and implemented within the organization. In our view leadership is not a core value in the traditional sense, but a technique or process that helps the business achieve its vision, mission, strategies, and core values. Thus, we have included the subject of leadership in the Appendix of this book. There is no right or wrong answer, but rather different perspectives and opinions. What do you think? ☺

#2 The *majority* of the material in this Appendix comes from chapter 4 in the book, *Choose Leadership*, in our Life Planning Series. If you want a more in-depth coverage of leadership you may want to supplement this subject with material from other chapters is that book [https://www.amazon.com/dp/1952359457].

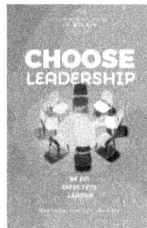

LEADERSHIP PRINCIPLES

A leadership principle is a fundamental rule, behavior, or policy that is intended to be followed. In a business organization these principles represent how the business will operate and how people are to lead and represent the organization. Leadership principles assure that both the leadership style of the organization and the leaders themselves are operating on sound concepts and techniques. They inherently direct leaders away from undesirable practices and behaviors.

Leadership principles are extremely important for the employer because they establish the tone and environment for the organization. They provide a common perspective for employees to do their best work. They produce an environment in which both leaders and employees have the same company perspectives.

If well-conceived leadership principles have been established, the organization can more accurately assess and measure performance. One cannot be held accountable for something that has not been clearly communicated. Thus, leadership principles are often part of the standard operating procedures of an organization. They may also be part of the company's Statement of Values.

Why do good organizations make a big deal out of leadership standards? Simply because they provide controls and a framework for doing business that will, in the opinion of the organization, provide the best opportunity for success in their business. Successful companies have demonstrated that establishing these principles is beneficial and will give an organization the best chance for success.

These principles inherently define what an organization values. They indicate what is important to the organization and how it intends to operate. The goal is to create the best environment for leaders and employees in order to provide customers with the best possible products and services. If quality is not an important value, products and services will tend to be overpriced. If customer service is not valued, customers will be frustrated when dealing with the company.

Leadership principles as well as core values apply to everyone in the organization because leadership is inherently the responsibility of all employees. This is true because everyone is a leader to some extent. No one, including the president or CEO, is exempt from these principles. These principles begin at the top and extend throughout the organization.

The principles create an environment that allows the organization to successfully compete in the marketplace. But the principles also help form and strengthen the character and capabilities of individual people. Good people doing good work produce good products that other people want to spend good money to acquire.

We have chosen the following principles because we believe they are the most important for good leadership. These are not in any particular order except for Principle #1 which we believe is the most critical to overall leadership success.

PRINCIPLE #1: COMMUNICATE WELL

A great leader must communicate effectively. But just communicating is not enough. Your communications must produce the desired result. Without good communication followers can be confused and misled. Frequent communication usually is a signal to followers that they are cared about and that their needs are important. Clear communication prevents misunderstandings. Open communication helps establish good ongoing dialogue between workers and management.

The leader must make sure his words clearly communicate his meaning and intent. It is important to allow followers to believe they are part of a team and doing something important to achieve common goals. The leader is part of a cohesive management team but he is the one with his hands on the wheel. The leader knows the goal and steers the team toward that goal using many techniques but effective communication is easily the most important.

Good leaders do not waste time with their communications. They communicate the information that keeps everyone informed and allows subordinates to make better decisions. Superfluous communication is kept to a minimum.

Good communication encourages followers to buy into the team goals. This allows them to participate in the success of the team and the organization. Both leaders and followers need to know the mission. Keeping everyone informed allows for their input and cooperation in achieving common goals. Poor communication can cause frustration and apathetic responses.

Good leaders communicate with humility. Instructions that are given in harsh and demanding styles will normally not be effective. Verbal instructions should be concise and should often be followed by written confirmation to avoid misunderstanding.

In today's workplace it is also necessary to be aware of different cultures when communicating with people or other companies. It is particularly important if you are operating in a global marketplace. Words often have different meanings in different cultures, therefore, chose your words carefully in a diverse marketplace.

Good leaders encourage subordinates to offer feedback and suggestions. The best communication is two-way to maximize clarity and cooperation. Effective communication going both up and down the chain of command is often the key to achieving common goals.

Leaders help team members understand where they fit in the organization, their importance, and what the future might look like. Good leaders paint a realistic picture of the future in order to excite employees about their work.

Communication to customers is critical to success. Most of the concepts mentioned above apply to communicating with your employees. Customers generally have the same needs as employees; only their perspective is different. If your product requires warnings they should be clear, concise, and well-crafted. Customer service should build its reputation on good and effective communication.

> *"You can have brilliant ideas, but if you can't get them across, your ideas won't get you anywhere."*
> Lee Iacocca, former CEO of Chrysler

PRINCIPLE #2: MANAGE CHANGE

Although we said that these leadership principles are not in any particular order, managing change may be nearly as important as communication. The one sure dynamic in this world is change. It will not stop or disappear. If you think it will then you will likely be the one to disappear. Recognizing and managing change is an absolute necessity for being a good leader. Understanding that the world is constantly changing will certainly impact your life and career.

Monitoring change is an essential activity if you expect any degree of competitive success.

In today's world if you cannot manage change you will not survive long. Technology is expanding at such a fast pace that if you are not adjusting to changes in your industry you will find yourself always playing catch-up. This world has no sympathy for people or organizations who fail to adapt and change.

Change is going to happen whether we want it or not. Therefore, good leaders do not fight change, but embrace it. They don't have time to grumble about it because they are figuring out how to make change work for them. Change can be a slow process or it can happen in a matter of weeks. It can be staggering and dramatic when there is a major paradigm shift.

Major change announces itself well in advance if we are listening! As I draft this chapter during the summer of 2023 the new life-changing technology on the horizon is artificial intelligence (AI). Artificial intelligence was cussed and discussed for years before it dramatically entered the market in a significant way in the fall of 2022 when ChatGPT was announced and made available to the public. Now there are multiple AI technologies available.

During the next 10 to 15 years our lives as individuals, family members, employees, and employers are going to undergo a mind-boggling paradigm shift because of AI. We have no idea of the scope and depth of the changes in front of us. Be prepared so that your lives and businesses are not left in the dust as massive change takes place.

Change can produce a number of good results:

- increased efficiency,
- more effectiveness,
- greater growth,
- high productivity, or
- greater profits.

Leaders with exceptional talent and above average foresight can often see change coming. They will be prepared to take advantage of change and use it to better their competition. Poor leaders see nothing and may resist the impact of change, finding it difficult to deal with in a dynamic and fluid environment. Being curious and innovative are, therefore, attractive traits for a leader in today's environment.

A major requirement for good leaders today is that they have adequate tech-savvy. If you do not understand the basics of today's technology, it will be more difficult for you to rise to any significant leadership level. In most organizations technology is an absolute requirement for business success and even survival. Thus, leaders must understand how it works, what it does, and how it can be used to improve their business. Existing leaders who don't possess adequate knowledge and understanding will be in danger of losing their jobs or simply reaching a point in an organization where they can no longer expect advancement.

Much is expected of leaders particularly during a time of dynamic change. They must be focused on market developments but they cannot forget the purpose and mission of their organization. A dynamic market place can place great stress on an organization. Good leaders often rise to the occasion during challenging times like this.

> *"Our future success is directly proportional to our ability to understand, adapt, and integrate new technology into our work."*
> Sukant Ratnakar

PRINCIPLE #3: LISTEN WELL

Employees want to be heard. Good leaders understand how important it is to listen well. When the leader listens, the team will listen. Listening goes both ways. Listening builds trust.

Customers also want to be heard! You can learn very valuable information by listening to your customers. If you make it hard to hear from customers you will not benefit from their good advice and likely suffer in the customer service area.

Leaders who fail to listen well will have a much more difficult time leading their team. Leaders must be able to hear ideas and suggestions as well as warnings of pending problems. Good leaders will ask the right questions to elicit constructive feedback. But if they are not listening well, they will miss critical information.

Employees want their leaders to listen to their ideas and be concerned about their needs. Leaders may not always accept or agree, but they do need to listen. Employees should make every attempt to ensure that their leaders understand what they are saying. But employees also want leaders to understand how they are feeling. If the leader demonstrates empathy and respect, listens well, and acknowledges input, both clients and employees will be satisfied.

Leaders who listen well will inherently make sure their team members that they understand the issues and problems. If the leader allows and evaluates input from their team, employees will line up behind whatever decision the leader ultimately makes. They will follow, not because they necessarily believe the leader made the right decision, but because their ideas were heard and considered.

Active listening is a quality that can prevent problems from happening or getting out of control. Workers on the front lines will frequently see issues and problems first and can be the key to fixing problems before they become critical. They will communicate this information when they know they are being heard. If the ears of team leaders are closed, many workers will simply allow problems to occur until they become obvious to the leader.

If leaders listen with sincere attention, trusting relationships will develop that benefit all members of the team. Active listening requires care and focus. This skill is sometimes the result of natural abilities, but if not, it must be developed by self-discipline and awareness.

"The roots of effective leadership lie in simple things, one of which is listening. Listening to someone demonstrates respect; it shows that you value their ideas and are willing to hear them."
John Baldoni

PRINCIPLE #4: DECISION-MAKING and PROBLEM-SOLVING

Good leaders are decisive. They do not shy away from problems and usually follow some form of recognized process in arriving at decisions. They never appear flustered or confused. They are confident in their decision-making because they take the necessary time to evaluate and analyze the available information.

Decision-makers acquire all the *available* data and information (although it may not be everything that exists) and then make a decision. Most good decisions can be made if the decision-maker has 60-80% of the available information.

Decisions are normally not made by committee. Good leaders evaluate the facts and then decide. Good leaders will exude confidence in their decisions, knowing that if the decision is wrong they will see the warning signs and fix the problem.

There is usually no clear cut alternative that you know is 100 percent right, and you will never get 100 percent of the information necessary to make a decision. Leaders recognize that any decision is temporary and can be modified at any time additional information becomes available indicating a change is necessary. They are prepared to move forward or change based on the information they have, knowing that delays and indecision are really a "do nothing" answer to the question or problem facing them.

Problem-solving

Good leaders work at being excellent problem-solvers. Roadblocks and difficulties are only temporary inconveniences. They will dig into problems with their team until the problem is identified and fixed. This skill may come naturally or be the result of training and education.

In today's workplace leaders must be skilled at solving problems because in this competitive marketplace any significant delay can be fatal. They must be able to make the very best decisions possible. Thus, problem-solving skills are crucial to being a good decision-maker. A leader who does not have these skills, or one whose skills are not the best, needs to have followers or associates that do.

Being decisive

Being decisive is a valuable skill and a characteristic of good leaders. It means that you make decisions in a reasonable amount of time. Your team is never on hold waiting for your decision. You are able to evaluate problems quickly and choose the right alternative among various possibilities in order to achieve the desired result. When decisions are delayed until all the information is obtained, the delay may negatively impact your competitive position in the marketplace.

Sometime being decisive is only a matter of knowledge and intelligence. At other times real wisdom is required to make the right choice. Failure to act and make a decision can often be as bad as making the wrong decision. Evaluate your options carefully and make a decision. That does not mean that you should be careless in order to make a quick decision. But once the situation has been adequately investigated, make a decision.

When the issues are clear and obvious it is easy to be decisive. But often you are faced with questions that have no obvious answer and no obvious solution is apparent. This is where good leaders will stand out among their peers. The good leader makes decisions knowing that he may need to change or shift his plans if new data indicates a change is necessary.

Outcomes are never guaranteed regardless of the amount of information available. Good leaders are comfortable making decisions in a fluid environment and willing to change on a dime if that decision proves inadequate or wrong.

Conclusion

Good decisions are not the result of guessing or good luck. They come about because of hard work and sometimes intense study. Wisdom and understanding must be able to take knowledge and apply it to the situation and develop good working solutions. New ideas and concepts always need to be investigated and evaluated.

Poor decision-making or ineffective thinking can create challenging competitive problems or bring an organization to its knees. Critical thinking, effective problem-solving, insightful planning, and effective execution of plans must be the expected role of good leadership.

Appendix C contains an outline of how to go about making good decisions. *If you need or want specific guidance on how to make good business decisions, review Appendix C.*

**Good leaders are skilled at
making decisions and solving problems!**

PRINCIPLE #5: LEAD BY EXAMPLE

Model the behavior you desire

The most productive teams often have leaders who are not afraid to work alongside their followers. They reflect in their work what they say in their talk. If a leader demonstrates a bad attitude, followers will usually follow suit. Leaders often get what they give.

Good leaders do not manage from afar and have little interaction with the work or the workers. Leaders are tuned into their people and know their successes as well as their problems. They will step in and assist when necessary. They will take time to explain and train. Good leaders want to achieve the best possible result and if that means spending time in the trenches, they will do it.

Actions usually speak much louder than words. Employees can see through speeches that mean nothing to the leader. A real leader earns trust and respect because he is engaged with the work. A leader's true character is demonstrated in what he does and not necessarily in what he says. Employees will quickly ignore the words of leaders that are not consistent with their corresponding actions or the purpose and mission of the organization.

Leaders demonstrate respect in the way they act toward workers. Leaders who lead by bluster and harsh words are quickly ignored and usually inspire only the minimum work and cooperation. Of course, that leads to more loud words, and the cycle may continue.

If you want good communications, then you must set the example. If you want an open atmosphere where all important issues are eligible for discussion, then you must be open to such. Secrets and topics that are off limits will not encourage an open and trusting environment.

Leading by example means the leader models the behavior she or he desires. The leader who wants respect must model courtesy, kindness, and encouragement. There are many ways to model the behavior you expect: be punctual, respect an employee's time, be an encourager, demonstrate kindness, dress appropriately, give credit to others for their work, be a good listener, etc.

Leaders do not have to be friends with their employees, but they do have to earn their respect and loyalty. Good leaders do not have to spend time making grand gestures intended to demonstrate their leadership ability; they must simply lead well. Good leaders are committed to the goals of the project and the company. Their actions should encourage workers to share that same commitment.

Patience, perseverance, and resilience

Patience generally means the act of bearing trials calmly, not complaining, and holding fast, even in the presence of opposition. Patient leaders do not make hasty decisions but they are persistent. They will persevere under whatever circumstances exist because they know that time is sometimes required to achieve goals.

Good leaders will not be deterred and if time is necessary to achieve interim objectives, they will be reasonably patient with mistakes, misunderstandings, and delays caused by others outside their control. But although they may be patient, their focus will not waver from priorities and commitments.

Leaders should demand excellence, but they must realize that excellence and patience can be difficult to balance. Good leaders never take their eyes off the goal. They have their focus on the big picture, knowing that it is the ultimate mission that must be achieved. Difficulties are battles that must be won in order to win the war.

Good leaders don't give up. They are resilient. They are in the game for the long term and know that achieving desired results does not always occur immediately. The situation may require new systems, new technology, or new people, none of which can occur quickly. They will not allow setbacks to deter them from achieving their goals. Resilient leaders are perceptive and know how to handle themselves in all situations. They will not be stopped by operational problems that must be resolved and overcome. They will maintain their focus and energy until the desired result is achieved.

Resilience is similar to perseverance but is usually meant to imply the ability to recover from misfortune. Employers value leaders who are patient, resilient, and able to persevere in challenging situations.

Resilient leaders are high performing
individuals who overcome challenges.

PRINCIPLE #6: SELF-CONFIDENCE

Self-confidence and intentionality can overcome the tendency to say "I can't" or "That's impossible for me." Walt Disney said, "It's kind of fun to do the impossible." This trait is a great motivator in accomplishing goals or fixing problems. Self-confidence means you trust yourself to accomplish a project or task. It does not necessarily mean that your first attempt will create the best solution, but you are not afraid to try. Generally people who have self-confidence are not concerned about failing. They know that if they do not succeed the first time, they will the second time, or the third.

Self-confidence is the trait of trusting in yourself, your knowledge, abilities, special skills, or judgment. This confidence is frequently a result of years of experience. It may also be the result of a mindset that wisdom and hard work will find good solutions.

Self-confidence can also result from a general feeling of trust in your analytical abilities to find solutions. You may not have any idea how to solve a particular problem but you are confident that you can follow a systematic approach to problem-solving and find a workable solution. Alternatively, you might have a very strong sense of confidence in an area where you have significant expertise or experience.

There are real benefits to being self-confident. The most important benefit may be that it usually results in better or higher performance. You are not afraid to take risks or make decisions and as a result you often produce creative and workable solutions. This may be the result of your ability to think outside the box and try new things. There is also a level of patience and perseverance that is an advantage to those who have confidence in their abilities.

Confidence combined with passion can be important motivators for accomplishing team goals or solving problems. Leaders who are confident are able to be decisive when decisions are required.

> *"You have to have confidence in your ability*
> *and be tough enough to follow through."*
> Rosalynn Carter

If you don't have confidence in your decisions or yourself, nobody else will either. Leaders must exhibit confidence even when they have questions in their own minds. How would you feel if your team leader made an important decision and then said he was not really confident it was going to work and hoped nobody would lose their jobs if the decision failed? If I were a team member, I would be getting my resume up-to-date.

In order to inspire followers or team members, a good leader will exude confidence in his and the organization's decisions. Uncertainty by the people required to carry out a decision can be a self-fulfilling prophecy. If you expect something to fail, it often will. If questions surround an undertaking, people will not want to be associated with something they think is suspect.

Good leaders will convince team members and anyone responsible for executing a decision that their best efforts are required. Leaders must inspire confidence and display certainty in their decisions. That attitude must be relayed to others along with an understanding of the bigger picture in order to assure subordinates the project is on track for success.

A good leader supports the purpose and mission of the organization. That attitude will be relayed down the chain of command and instill belief in what is to be accomplished. Troubles occur when the purpose, mission, or plan are not explicitly clear. Workers can see through half-hearted support and if it is not addressed, such doubt can ambush a project before it even gets started.

Communications are critically important in the midst of important decisions because innocent misunderstandings can create doubt and fear. If lower level leaders believe that decisions are not aligned with the organization's stated goals or values, confidence must be restored. All levels of management must feel comfortable asking questions up the chain-of-command if they have serious questions or doubts.

The "what" to be done is certainly necessary for critical decisions, but so is the "why." If the people implementing change do not know the "why," they often have little confidence in the "what" they are doing. Leaders at _all_ levels must understand the purposes behind decisions so they can wholeheartedly support them.

> *"Leaders must be tough enough to fight,*
> *tender enough to cry, human enough to make*
> *mistakes, humble enough to admit them,*
> *strong enough to absorb the pain,*
> *and resilient enough to bounce back*
> *and keep on moving."*
> Jesse Jackson

PRINCIPLE #7: LOYALTY / COMMITMENT TO COMPANY

Good leaders act like owners. Nothing is beyond their interest. Everything is important because they want the organization to succeed. They inherently take on the responsibility of an owner and tend to think of themselves as ambassadors of the organization.

Leaders must commit to the organization. They must want the organization to succeed and be determined to work fully and completely toward that goal. Committed leaders feel personally responsible for the success of the organization. They will work tirelessly to make the business successful.

But leaders do not lead by themselves. They have followers. Good leaders build teams and relationships that allow more effective work habits and ultimately better results. People want connections. They need to feel that they are valued, trusted, and cared for. Developing good interpersonal relationships with team members helps build lasting connections that become invaluable when the work is particularly demanding.

Leaders are responsible for producing the end result. They are responsible for keeping the focus on the purpose and mission of the organization. The goal of any team must ultimately be to produce quality products or services that are consistent with the mission and vision of the organization.

Core values

Although Core Values are a foundation for everyone, they are particularly important for leaders and the organization. Leaders must have personal core values that drive their work, moral standards, and reputation. They also represent the core values of the company. Employees will be encouraged to share the core values of the organization, but they may not necessarily hold to those values as strongly as the leaders and the organization.

If employees hold similar values it will create harmony and often reduce the likelihood of confusion over instructions or motives. Leaders may hold employees to the company standards, even to the point of asking people to leave if they violate company core values.

These values create and maintain the culture of the group or company. Leaders do not want confusion about core values to linger or create divided loyalties. If there is a problem with expectations, the leader must address it immediately.

A leader cannot allow company core values to be ignored or put aside by employees. If that happens it will appear the leader doesn't really adhere to either his personal core values or those of the organization. Non-compliance with core values can dramatically impact the performance and cohesion of a group, while destroying the purposes or goals of the organization.

Good leaders will implement policies that benefit the entire team and are consistent with the core values of the organization. They may work individually with employees or teach and motivate group members. Leaders want everyone to know their role as it relates to their contribution to the work and how that harmonizes with the purposes of the company.

Demand for excellence

One major short-coming of some leaders or companies is that they accept poor or sub-standard performance. This usually means that the ultimate product or service is also substandard. Everyone, including the leader, must be held accountable for poor performance. Standards must be enforced. Excellence must be required and substandard work must be rejected. If not, the result can ultimately cause the company to fail. Quality work and commitment to company core values should be demanded as a necessary job performance characteristic.

Leaders know the mission

One of the most important qualities of a leader is that he knows and supports the purpose and mission of the organization. Everything a leader says and does should be tested against the mission.

Senior leaders think big, see the business in terms of its mission, and inspire others to fulfill the purpose. Thinking small, local, and always within the boundaries will not allow the organization to "go where no one has gone before." Senior leaders inspire and communicate their vision for the express purpose of achieving company strategic goals.

PRINCIPLE #8: PLANNING

Planning, prioritizing, organizing, and executing are the most basic and fundamental responsibilities of a good leader. The success of a leader is often determined by how well he plans and prioritizes. To implement and execute effectively a leader must:

- Know what is important and attack the high priority problems first.

- Develop a plan of action that is clear and concise; one that everyone on the team can understand and follow.
- Adequately analyze the situation and develop solutions with the help of team members and trusted advisors.
- Manage and oversee execution of the plan, ensuring that the critical focus is on high priority tasks.
- Regularly review progress and confirm that priorities have not changed.
- Communicate status up and down the chain of command.

If there are many problems or multiple projects, managing for results can be stressful and overwhelming. Plans must be monitored with team members so that everyone knows what is important, where the projects are going, and how well they are doing. If there are numerous critically important issues at stake, the environment can be very tense and stress can impact the entire team. Priorities can sometimes change resulting in a plan that changes frequently.

Good leaders will not become rattled in a high-stakes situation. They will demonstrate a calm demeanor and attention to detail. In these situations good communication is vital for all team members. The more the entire team understands the more likely it is that the focus will remain on high priority issues and not be sidelined chasing unimportant issues. It is sometimes easy to get overly focused on one particular issue if no one is looking at the whole picture.

Good leaders make necessary refinements in plans as clear and concise as possible. In addition, when the mission changes, that must be quickly and effectively communicated to team members so that the work does not lose focus or become ineffective. When everyone understands the mission it is much easier to make good decisions. Battling misunderstanding or rebellion simply wastes resources.

Planning is needed at all levels of a project. Executives make the broad directives and pass those down the chain of command. The planning process continues at all levels of the organization. There should be a common purpose, mission, and goal guiding the planning process. The more junior leaders participate in the process the easier it will be to implement change with the front-line team members because they will take ownership of the plan. Employees who understand the purpose and vision find it easier to accept the reason for changes.

The best teams and leaders will frequently monitor progress. Is the plan being implemented properly and is it producing the expected results? A progress review will often ask questions such as:

- What is working? Are the results as projected?
- What is not working? Why?
- What new issues have arisen because of the changes?
- What have we learned that should trigger other changes?

PRINCIPLE #9: DELEGATION

Because leaders cannot do everything themselves, they must learn to delegate. Often delegation is necessary because someone has special and unique knowledge or capabilities that will assure a better result. Leaders consider the following in delegating responsibility:

- who is highly skilled,
- should another team member learn this skill/work,
- should the work be recurring,
- should it be assigned permanently, or
- what is the time frame for the work?.

Delegated responsibility must be accompanied by associated authority. Responsibility without authority is a losing proposition. Typically nothing happens if the authority does not exist to make something happen. Frustration will occur when subordinates without authority are held responsible for results they cannot impact.

The more effectively delegation is accomplished, the more likely it is that a leader and his team will be successful. Delegation is more than just assigning work – it is giving responsibility and authority to the right person because he or she has the ability to do the job. The result should be that team performance and productivity is improved.

Delegation gives the right work to the right person
for the right reasons to produce the right result.

Great leaders empower their teams to achieve or exceed goals. Leaders must rely on good people to do good work. Otherwise the leader must do it all and that is never possible. The leader must train subordinates to take responsibility for managing the process to achieve team goals. Likewise subordinates must be prepared to use their skills and capabilities to achieve team solutions and goals.

Empowering team members to develop and use their talents will build a strong team that will be effective when their skills are needed to overcome difficulties. If the leader does not develop this capability in his team, it will be much more difficult to overcome problems.

Good leaders manage teams to deliver projects completed on time, within or under budget, and be of the highest quality possible. They manage difficulties and problems until they are overcome. They make no excuses. Thus, delegation becomes a highly effective form of team management in order to produce excellent results.

PRINCIPLE #10: MOTIVATE and INSPIRE

Emotions

Employees will not follow leaders who show no emotion or passion. Good leaders are invested in their responsibilities and demonstrate passion and emotion in inspiring others to achieve results.

Good leaders harness the emotions of their team members to produce the very best result possible. People who suggest that emotion does not belong in the workplace don't understand the human condition. Emotions are everywhere within the work environment. How they are displayed will depend on the person and the work environment. Positive emotions can be very beneficial in most work situations.

A good working team will often be a very close knit unit. Emotions can arise because the work is important and the people are invested in the success of the work and in each other.

A good leader uses both head and heart knowledge in managing his team. It is important to be sensitive to feelings, perceptions, points of view, new ideas, or anything that might create stress and anxiety.

Inspire others

Leaders provide inspiration so that others can find meaning in a vision or purpose. Without meaning and inspiration those who follow will often have a difficult time committing themselves to the greater purpose. Inspiration helps people see that what they do matters.

Subordinates need to know that their management has a clear vision and purpose. They want to know that the business is stable and have faith that their leaders are guiding them in the right direction. Good leaders will present a positive image, communicate hope, and encourage others to feel good about what they are doing.

PRINCIPLE #11: TRUST

Good leaders delegate responsibilities to their trusted junior leaders. A leader will trust the team to carry out normal and special projects. Delegation demonstrates trust in subordinates and that trust will normally go both up and down the chain of command.

Great teams are built on trust and cooperation. If you cannot completely trust your partner, your team members, your family, or your co-workers, everything will probably fall apart. Trust is the cement that holds all relationships together. When trust is lost, high performance teams, no matter how skilled, will lose their edge and probably fail.

Trust is a critical aspect of leadership. A leader must be trusted by the team to make good decisions, communicate honestly, and deliver on his promises. If subordinates do not trust the decisions or actions of the leader it will be difficult for the leader to marshal the cooperation and commitment to tackle the job.

Honesty and truth are generally considered the number one requirements for garnering trust in any group situation. A lack of honesty will not only reflect poorly on the leader but will also reflect back on the organization. If the leader or management personnel are not trustworthy, then it is unlikely that the organization is any better.

Practices that help build trust:

1. Work together

Good leaders will interact with and often participate in the daily activities of the team. Employees benefit greatly by interacting with leaders. Demonstrating that you want your subordinates to develop in their careers will open lines of communication and also indicate you value their input and opinions.

2. Give others credit

Always recognize the accomplishments of the team and team members. Give credit to the team when there are successes and take responsibility for mistakes and problems. Never publically call out the team for criticism. Discuss problems in private. Always put the team first and yourself second.

3. Demonstrate mutual respect

If you want to receive loyalty and trust you must earn respect and trust. Mutual respect is a foundation for trust. Sharing and openness without negative talk and complaining will help create an environment of trust. Gossip, grumbling, dishonesty, or insincerity will never create a foundation of mutual respect.

4. Admit mistakes

As a leader, you become real to your subordinates when you admit errors, mistakes, or poor judgment. Failure is not necessarily a good thing, but it can be used to gain understanding and build better working relationships. Sincerity and truth require that you not only admit mistakes but demonstrate how to deal with setbacks on a positive basis. The best way to discourage hiding mistakes is to demonstrate that the focus around mistakes is finding solutions, not casting blame.

5. Maintain high personal values

People trust others who stay true to their personal core values and the standards of the organization. Maintaining core values will create respect and trust in a team or organization.

6. Servant leadership

Servant leadership is often at the core of building a trust relationship with employees. Putting the team first will create two-way communication that helps establish a mindset of respect. Successful leaders give without necessarily expecting anything in return, other than cooperation, diligence, and a helpful attitude.

Trust must exist up and down the chain of command. The blame game can destroy an organization. Leaders and workers should be unified by a common goal. Hidden agendas destroy the ability to be successful. Transparency and communication are trademarks of an atmosphere where trust is paramount.

Open conversations and honest feedback facilitate trusting relationships. Thoughts, feelings, beliefs, and ideas can be shared openly in this kind of environment.

CONCLUSION

Leadership principles must be carefully considered and balanced in order to ensure that the best outcome is achieved for the organization. Serious leadership challenges can occur when leaders rely too heavily on one leadership principle to the detriment of others. Excellent leadership requires that a leader be skilled in a number of skills and techniques in order to meet the needs of both employees and the organization.

EXERCISE #1 – Leadership Case Study Analysis

Objective: Analyze real-life leadership scenarios to understand the impact of quality leadership on organizational success.

Instructions:
a. Select a few case studies that highlight different aspects of leadership and its impact on workplace dynamics and outcomes. You can find these in business books, journals, magazines, or the internet.

b. Divide employees into small groups and provide each group with a different case study.

c. Instruct the groups to read and discuss the case study, analyzing the leadership actions and their consequences.

d. Encourage participants to identify key leadership traits, behaviors, or decisions that contributed to positive outcomes or challenges within the case study.

e. Have each group present their findings, insights, and conclusions to the larger group.

f. Facilitate a group discussion, drawing connections between the case studies and the importance of quality leadership in fostering a productive and effective workforce.

g. Encourage participants to reflect on how they can apply these lessons to their own roles and interactions within the organization.

EXERCISE #2 – Leadership Skills Workshop

Objective: Provide practical skills-building exercises to enhance participants' leadership abilities.

Instructions:
a. Organize a workshop or training session focused on developing leadership skills.

b. Identify key leadership competencies or skills relevant to your organization (e.g., effective communication, decision-making, team building, etc.).

c. Break participants into smaller groups and assign each group a specific leadership skill to work on.

d. Provide relevant resources, such as articles, case studies, or videos, to guide their learning.

e. Instruct each group to develop a short presentation or demonstration showcasing their assigned leadership skill.

f. Allocate time for groups to practice and prepare their presentations.

g. Have each group present their findings to the larger group, highlighting the importance of their assigned leadership skill.

h. Facilitate a discussion to consolidate the key takeaways and encourage participants to reflect on how they can apply these skills in their roles as leaders or aspiring leaders.

i. Consider providing additional resources or follow-up activities to support ongoing leadership development.

Appendix C – Decision-Making

*"Unintended consequences rush us recklessly
through life, allowing no time for perspective."*
(Unknown)

Special note: This Appendix is similar to Chapter 9 in *CHOOSE Leadership*, in our Life Planning Series. A similar version of this subject can also be obtained as a 99 cent eBook (Kindle) at:
https://www.amazon.com/dp/B09SYGWRVL/

We feel that decision-making is a key skill that needs to be included in this book and taught to employees. The eBook copy is more focused on making *personal* life choices. In this Appendix the focus is on making decisions in a business/project environment.

MAKING SOUND DECISIONS

Decision-making and problem-solving are essential work and career skills. Making good decisions is not that hard if you can think through all the reasonable alternatives. Unfortunately, we often do not spend adequate time thinking! Can we always get it right? No! But we can significantly improve our ability to make good choices.

One of the biggest reasons anyone struggles in making decisions is fear. You may have fear of the unknown, failure, or missing out on something better. You must not allow these fears to paralyze you. Making *no* decision may be the worst choice you can make.

We often avoid the most obvious solution: *thinking!*

The Academics of Decision-Making

Most standard textbooks on the subject of decision-making condense the process down to four to eight key steps. For example:

1. **Clarify the Issue:** What is the problem? How can it be identified or described? What is the real decision that must be made?

2. **Gather the Data:** Before you can do anything you must gather relevant data about the issue or problem from all available sources.

3. **Possible Alternatives:** What are the reasonable actions that might be taken to resolve the issue? What are the viable alternatives? What will the alternatives produce? How risky are the options?

4. **Best Choice:** Which alternatives produce the best risk/reward solutions? Select the best alternative given your situation.

5. **Implement:** Implement your choice.

6. **Monitor:** Regularly review your progress.

These are the basic steps in making most decisions. The key to any method is to approach the problem in an organized manner and logically consider the actions that might be taken. Then choose the best one given your situation and the organization's penchant for risk.

You can make decisions in a number of different ways. Sometimes it's simply instinct or intuition. You just know or feel what the right thing is to do. Others gather data and information, filling notebooks with everything they can think of that would help determine the right choice. Some of us make a check list of questions and answers before we decide. And, finally, there is the trusted "pros and cons" approach.

RECOMENDATION: We suggest an analytical approach for making business decisions. This requires looking at a number of important issues before making a decision. Some of these issues and questions may not apply to every question or to your particular situation. Just ignore those and focus on the questions that are pertinent.

The Short and Sweet Method

For those of you who must make this process short and sweet, the answers to the following three questions <u>may</u> be adequate for you to make a good decision.

1. Should the organization do it or not do it? Why? Why not?
2. What are the detailed pros and cons?
3. What is the best alternative given the pros and cons?

There is really nothing inherently wrong with the "short and sweet" method, but we do not recommend it for serious business decisions. The key in this method is identifying all the important pros and cons. If you are not sure you have thought of everything, consider a more detailed approach as follows.

Experience

Your previous experience and the experience of others can be invaluable in making good decisions. Often you can avoid mistakes by learning from the experience of someone else. Find a trusted experienced person and ask their opinion. For example, talk to a retired manager or supervisor from your area.

The experienced person may have first-hand experience in what you are facing. There may be pitfalls you know nothing about. This concept is true for many decisions – talk to someone who has already experienced the problem. What did they do and how did it turn out?

> *"The most difficult thing is the decision to act,*
> *the rest is merely tenacity. The fears are paper tigers.*
> *You can do anything you decide to do.*
> *You can act to change and control your life;*
> *and the procedure, the process is its own reward."*
> Amelia Earhart

A to Z Decision-making Process

GENERAL

A. Confidence. Be confident but never assume every idea will work. Don't look at everything through rose-colored glasses.

B. The Problem. Sometimes it is easy to misdiagnose the situation. Have you correctly identified the problem? Do you know what is happening and why, or are you just guessing?

C. Focus. Stay focused on the problem. Keep your eye on the issue at hand. Don't become distracted and try to solve some other problem. Know what you want to achieve and focus on that result.

D. Mistakes. Don't worry about making mistakes. Everyone makes them, and they often occur at the most inopportune times. If they occur, the focus should be on fixing the problem, not casting blame.

LEGAL/ETHICAL

E. Core values. Never violate your core values or the values of the employer. Don't even consider something that would compromise your standards. If you have a sense that you are doing something wrong, stop and consider what is really going to happen if you proceed. Don't allow anger, fear, feelings, or emotions to convince you to do something that you know is wrong.

RESEARCH

F. Information. You need information and good data in order to make good decisions. You cannot even begin thinking about solutions until you know the facts. Make sure that the data you gather is valid and applicable to your situation.

ANALYSIS

G. Situation. Look at your situation from different viewpoints. Don't lock yourself into just one frame of reference. From what different viewpoints might you consider the issues and what are the impacts? Ask yourself what would happen if you did the opposite of what you are considering. What would happen if you did nothing?

H. Cost. Ask yourself what this decision will cost in dollars, relationships, or missed opportunities. Know the cost of <u>not</u> making a decision (which is a decision itself). Cost should be part of your risk/reward evaluation.

I. Impact. What is going to happen? What other events will be set into motion? What will others think about the quality of this decision? Will you receive support or criticism?

EVALUATION

J. Think. Make sure you take adequate time to fully consider the issues and your proposed solutions. But don't overthink it. If you begin to overthink the question you can end up going down a lot of time-consuming and irrelevant rabbit trails. It is easy to lose focus if you continually review the same material again and again.

K. Importance. Know the importance of the decision in the overall scheme of things. Don't waste time mulling over a decision that has no real value. Assign a dollar value if that is possible. What are the potential good or bad results that cannot be easily quantified?

L. Prioritize. Every decision you make should be measured against organizational values, priorities, or goals. Make sure you know what is important. Don't waste time and effort considering changes that have very little importance.

M. Risks. Make sure you know the real underlying risks you are taking. Who or what will be impacted by your choices and how will they be affected? Compare what could be lost against what could be gained. Is the risk worth it? What happens if the situation must be abandoned? What could you do up front to reduce the risk?

N. Future. Make sure you think about both the short-term and long-term impact of your decisions. Something that is very good in the short term may be very bad in the long term.

O. Break down big decisions. It is often easier to make a number of small decisions than one really big one. If you are faced with a big and presumably serious decision, break it down into its component parts. It is much easier to make smaller decisions that accumulate into one big one than to tackle the entire problem.

P. Timing. Poor timing can make some decisions very difficult to implement or achieve. If you are dealing with a timing situation, re-evaluate your options to stop, slow down, or go forward.

DECISION-MAKING

Q. Advisors. We all have trusted friends, mentors, and advisors whom we could ask for feedback. Get their advice, but understand that in the end, you must make the decision. This is not a committee taking a vote. You are responsible.

R. Emotions. Don't allow emotions to sway your decisions because the result could be disastrous. On the other hand, don't totally ignore them either. Understand the role emotions play in your personal or business decision-making process.

S. Fear. Fear of making a mistake or of incurring bad consequences can sometimes prevent people from making any decision at all. Don't freeze up worrying about all the possible consequences. Get help. Get advice. Get moving. Don't be paralyzed by fear.

T. Extremes. Be reasonable in projecting into the future. Examine any history that is available. Is a good middle-of-the-road approach a viable choice? Beware of the extremes.

U. Instincts. Sometime instincts are valid but most of the time they are not good ways to make decisions. Instinct may work if you are seasoned in the subject and have made successful decisions in this area in the past.

V. Thinking. Don't spend all your time thinking. At some point the thinking must turn into doing. Spend adequate time thinking and analyzing the situation. When there is nothing more to think about, it is time for a decision.

W. Alternatives. Limit the options you are considering to those that have a reasonable chance of success. That will usually be 2 to 4 possibilities. Recheck your thinking and move forward with the best alternative available. If a better solution is identified at a later time, make the necessary adjustments. There is nothing wrong with changing your mind if a better solution becomes evident.

IMPLEMENTAION

X. Slow speed ahead. Implement your solutions slowly enough that you know what is working and what is not. Give your solutions time to succeed or fail. Don't rush to judgment. Don't try to implement too much too soon such that you lose control of the situation.

Y. Change direction. You can never know in advance or be sure that a particular decision will be correct. There is some risk in every alternative. Be prepared to take risks, and be prepared to fix problems or change direction if the results dictate the solution is not working.

Z. Stay the course. Once you have made your decision, stick with it unless you have clear evidence that you are on the wrong path. Don't change your mind because you get cold feet or have about of anxiety.

> *"You are free to choose, but the choices*
> *you make today will determine what you*
> *have, be, and do in the tomorrow of your life."*
> Zig Ziglar

TEN DETAILED STEPS TO GOOD DECISIONS

1. DEFINE IT: Obtain all the necessary information and state the question or problem in a simple clear sentence or two.

> a. Gather the information necessary to make the decision. Know the facts and the history. You will never get 100% of the information – 70% to 80% is pretty good.
> b. Know the timeline and time requirements of the decision.
> c. What is the *real* problem or issue? Define it correctly and completely. What do you have to decide?
> d. Don't avoid or ignore any facts. Do your homework and research well.
> e. Define the problem, opportunity, or decision. Write it down for clarity and perspective.

2. LEGAL/ETHICAL: Does this decision involve any legal issues, ethical standards, moral boundaries, or company policies? Clarify in detail.

> a. Would it violate society's laws or the organization's core values or policies?
> b. Is this a question of right versus wrong or pushing ethical boundaries in any way? Explain.
> c. Will the organization be proud of the outcome?

3. CONSEQUENCES: What are the consequences? Can I live with them? Who and what will be affected, influenced, or impacted?

> a. What is the impact on my team and the organization? Does this create unreasonable expectations for me or others?

b. Will this decision help or hurt the team or the organization?
c. Will this decision or solution change lives? How?
d. How will this feel in 6 months, in 12 months, in 24 months?
e. What is the short and long-term impact? Am I likely to make the same decision if I wait two weeks or two months?
f. If I can't please everyone, who must I please in this situation?   Co-workers - Organization - Investors
g. Count the <u>cost</u>! Just because it feels right or seems like the thing to do, it may not fit with the time schedule, available resources, or skills of team members

4. FINANCIAL RISKS and REWARDS: What are the risks and rewards? What can we gain or lose? Are the risks reasonable?

a. What resources do I need? Can I acquire the necessary resources at a reasonable cost?
b. What is the worst case scenario? How likely is it? Could I live with that? Can the organization afford to lose what is invested?
c. Am I being realistic?

5. EXPERTISE: Do I have the skills and ability to make this decision?

a. Do I need additional wisdom, advice, skill, information, or experience to make this decision?
b. Do I have or can I obtain the necessary expertise and resources to accomplish this goal or project?
c. Who should be making this decision? Is it me or not me?
d. Do I have the authority to make this decision?

6. ADVISORS: Seek out advisors for intelligent and honest advice.

a. Seek out <u>trusted</u> advisors who are trustworthy, capable, intelligent, and diverse. They must have my interests at heart, and not be "yes" men.
b. <u>Listen</u> (really listen) to their advice. What do they think? What is their counsel? What is their logic and reasoning?
c. Do my friends and advisors agree or are they divided or conflicting? Why? What's the issue?

    d. Don't permit the advisors to make the decision! Advisors may have their own or a different agenda!

7. CONSIDERATIONS: Is it consistent with my core values and the values of the organization? Are my motives right? Am I being influenced by feelings, emotions, fears, or insecurities?

    a. CORE VALUES:
- Does this conflict with the organization's core values or policies in any way?
- Is it just and fair (morally right)?

    b. GOALS:
- How does this fit with the organization's short and long-term business goals?

    c. PASSION:
- What emotions are impacting this decision? They should not override good judgment!

    d. MOTIVES:
- What are my motives? Do I have any hidden agendas? Am I trying to fool myself?
- Are there selfish or unworthy ambitions involved? Is pride or arrogance present?
- Am I doing something for the wrong reasons?

    e. FEELINGS:
- Feelings may be very deceptive and can lead to undesirable results.
- Do not be influenced by the age-old concept of "I feel good about it."

    f. FEARS:
- What are my inherent fears and how are they influencing my decision?
- Fears cannot be allowed to dictate decisions, but they should be evaluated.
- Do I feel pressured? What is that pressure? Why does it exist?

8. ALTERNATIVE SOLUTIONS: Take time to fully analyze the information in order to make a fully informed decision.

    a. Analyze the information and develop all <u>viable</u> solutions.
    b. Think outside the box. Expand the solutions.
    c. Look at the problem from a different viewpoint.
    d. Reduce the options down to the 2 most viable alternatives.

9. DECIDE: Verify the facts and consider the solution, then decide.

    a. VERIFY: Verify the facts as necessary. Confirm the opinions of your advisors and settle in for some thinking.

    b. SIMPLIFY: Make it simple. Don't make it more complicated.

    c. THINK: Think about the solution. Spend time evaluating the tough issues surrounding this decision. Don't allow problems or unknowns to frustrate you. Big decisions are hard work!

    d. TIME: How much of my time will be required? Can we do this in the required time-frame?

    e. RIGHT: Is it fair, equitable, and just? By this point you should have eliminated anything that is illegal, violates core values, or is against your company's rules and polices.

    f. ANALYSIS PARALYSIS: Don't overthink it. Don't be afraid to make a decision. If the result ends up being wrong, then accept the mistake, correct it, and move on.

    g. ADVISORS: Would others (my advisors) in my situation make the same decision? Why? Why not?

    h. SOCIAL MEDIA: How will social media react to this decision? Do I need to be ready to respond? Do I care?

    i. RUSH: If I am being <u>*forced*</u> to make an immediate answer or choice, then the answer is probably NO!

    j. SUSTAINABLE: Is the decision a permanent solution? Will I be facing the same issues again in several months?

k. SAYING NO: It's okay to say no! If it's not right, it's not right.

l. DELAY: Not making a decision is a decision. No decision is choosing the status quo.

m. PERFECT DECISIONS: There is no such thing as a perfect decision. Are you generally comfortable and content with your decision? If not, more study and analysis may be necessary, or the answer may be "no."

n. DECIDE: Decide and move forward.

10. AFTERWARD: Monitor the situation closely so that the intended result occurs. Take corrective action as needed.

a. How will I monitor the results? How will I know if there are problems?
b. Who do I go to with questions if difficulties arise?
c. Doubts are common. Make sure they are valid. Don't ignore them, but don't let them get out of hand. Don't allow problems or difficulties to automatically raise doubts.

CONCLUSION

Some organizations may want certain of their core values weighted more highly in making company decisions. Leaders should understand how the factors they are considering relate to the values of the company. Certain issues may need to be weighted more or less given the values and goals of the organization. For example, if the organization is very conservative and desires to follow the lead of other major competitors, suggesting a solution that puts the company on the leading edge of technology is not likely the right alternative.

> *"The success of an organization is directly proportional to the quality of its decision-making."*
> John C. Maxwell

Improve your life!

Life Planning Handbook

Obtain a copy of the Handbook if you want to be guided in developing your own personal Life Plan.

Purpose of a Life Plan

- To help you develop direction in your life.
- To encourage you to make good decisions.
- To help build your life on proven life principles.
- To help you establish goals for your life.
- To identify what you hope to accomplish in life.
- To help you make the most of every opportunity.

Life Planning
Series

Life Planning
Handbook

Go to https://www.amazon.com/dp/1952359325
to get your copy now.

Don't wait to have a better life!

Life Planning Series

Read these books if you want to live a better life.

LIFE PLANNING HANDBOOK	**A Life Plan will shape your life journey!** The next step in your life planning.
CHOOSE INTEGRITY	**Life Principle:** Be honest, live with integrity, and base your life on truth.
CHOOSE FRIENDS WISELY	**Life Principle:** Choose your friends wisely.
CHOOSE THE RIGHT WORDS	**Life Principle:** Guard your speech.
CHOOSE GOOD WORK HABITS	**Life Principle:** Be diligent and a hard worker.
CHOOSE FINANCIAL RESPONSIBILITY	**Life Principle:** Make sound financial choices.

CHOOSE A POSITIVE SELF-IMAGE	**Life Principle:** Be confident in who you are.
CHOOSE LEADERSHIP	**Life Principle:** Lead well and be a loyal follower.
CHOOSE CORE VALUES	**Life Principle:** Core values will drive your life.
CHOOSE LOVE AND FAMILY	**Life Principle:** Build strong relationships.
CHOOSE FAITH	*Your Spiritual Guidebook for Questions about Religion, God, Heaven, Truth, Evil, and the Afterlife.*

Go to: **https://www.amazon.com/dp/B09TH9SYC4**

to get your copy.

Acknowledgments

My wife has patiently persevered while I indulged my interest in this subject. Thank you for your patience.

Our older daughter has been an invaluable resource. She has also graciously produced our website at www.lifeplanningtools.com. Our middle daughter designed the covers for this series and this book. We are very grateful for her help, talent and creativity.

Notes

Use of Artificial Intelligence (AI)

The author has made some use of AI for outlines, research, and initial drafts of information for some portions of this book. The author does not claim any specific original thought on the subject of core values – they have existed since the beginning of time. The focus of this book is to define and describe the nature of existing core values and suggest how they might be used by an organization in their business in order to gain competitive advantage. Therefore the focus is on how to train employees and implement core value strategies within the organization. The only use of AI that was not extensively re-written was the "Exercises" at the end of each chapter and some of the "Practical Tips."

Use of Quotes

ACCURACY: We have used a number of quotes throughout this book that came from our files, notes, books, public articles, the Internet, etc. We have made no attempt to verify that these quotes were actually written or spoken by the person they are attributed to. Regardless of the source of these quotes, the wisdom of the underlying message is relative to the content in this book and worth noting, even if the source reference is erroneous.

SOURCE: Unless otherwise specifically noted below the quotes used herein can be sourced from a number of different websites on the Internet that provide lists of quotes by subject or author. The same or similar quotes will appear on multiple sites. The sources for the quotes used in this book include:

azquotes.com	graciousquotes.com	quotir.com
brainyquote.com	inc.com	success.com
codeofliving.com	keepinspiring.me	thoughtco.com
everydaypower.com	notable-quotes.com	thoughtcatalog.com
goalcast.com	parade.com	wisdomquotes.com
goodhousekeeping.com	plantetofsuccess.com	wisesayings.com
goodreads.com/quotes	quotemaster.org	wow4u.com

Footnotes For Illustration Stories

A Johnson & Johnson Tylenol Crisis (Integrity):
    (a) https://time.com/3423136/tylenol-deaths-1982/;
    (b) https://ourstory.jnj.com/tylenol%C2%AE-tampering-incidents-and-recall;
    (c) https://www.investopedia.com/ask/answers/011215/how-did-johnson-and-johnsons-corporate-responsibility-policy-pay-1982.asp.

B Toyota (Quality):
    (a) https://www.hillfordglobal.com/post/driven-to-succeed-the-inspiring-story-of-toyota-s-rise-to-global-dominance;
    (b) https://primeinsights.in/success-story-of-toyota/;
    (c) https://www.cascade.app/studies/how-toyota-went-from-humble-beginnings-to-automotive-giant.

C Amazon Customer-oriented):
    (a) https://aws.amazon.com/executive-insights/content/the-imperatives-of-customer-oriented-innovation/;
    (b) https://www.bbc.com/news/business-55927979;
    (c) https://www.powerreviews.com/blog/amazon-customer-oriented-strategy/.

D Netflix (Results-oriented)
    (a) https://www.bbc.co.uk/news/business-55723926
    (b) https://www.theceomagazine.com/business/management-leadership/netflix/

E Warby Parker (Innovation)
    (a) https://leaders.com/articles/leaders-stories/warby-parker/
    (b) https://blog.hubspot.com/marketing/warby-parker-business-lessons
    (c) https://www.sipa.columbia.edu/news/warby-parker-cofounder-discusses-entrepreneurship-social-mission

F SpaceX (Teamwork)
    (a) https://bstrategyhub.com/spacex-mission-statement-vision-core-values-analysis/
    (b) https://hbr.org/2021/05/high-performing-teams-start-with-a-culture-of-shared-values
    (c) https://www.forbes.com/sites/forbestechcouncil/2021/12/21/effective-collaboration-is-crucial-to-high-employee-engagement/

G1 Google (Employee development)
    (a) https://www.tituslearning.com/how-google-does-learning-and-development/
    (b) https://www.mollearn.com/about/news/talent-google-learning-loo-and-so-much-more/
    (c) https://www.trainingzone.co.uk/community/blogs/alexk/how-google-creates-impactful-employee-training

G2 HubSpot (Employee development)
    (a) https://blog.hubspot.com/the-hustle/employee-development
    (b) https://blog.hubspot.com/blog/tabid/6307/bid/33282/The-Ultimate-Guide-to-Creating-Compelling-Case-Studies.aspx
    (c) https://blog.hubspot.com/customers/education-academy-certifications-grow-train-team

H Ford Motor Company (Accountability)
    (a) https://www.kornferry.com/insights/briefings-magazine/issue-20/alan-mulally-man-who-saved-ford
    (b) https://real-leaders.com/stories/leadership/the-leadership-style-that-turned-ford-motor-company-around/
    (c) https://strategicdiscipline.positioningsystems.com/blog-0/cadence-of-accountability-how-alan-mulally-rid-ford-of-poor-performers

I   Starbucks (Respect)
      (a) https://stories.starbucks.com/stories/2020/our-commitment-to-inclusion-diversity-and-equity-at-starbucks/
      (b) https://platformmagazine.org/2021/03/26/starbucks-the-pr-tactics-in-inclusivity/
      (c) https://stories.starbucks.com/press/2020/milestones-starbucks-efforts-to-support-racial-justice-and-equity/

J1 Patagonia, Volkswagen, BP Oil, Wells Fargo (Social responsibility)
      (a) https://eu.patagonia.com/hr/en/social-responsibility.html.
      (b) https://www.patagonia.com/social-responsibility/.
      (c) https://www.chuckjoe.co/patagonia-corporate-social-responsibility/.
      (d) https://woodwardavenue.org/patagonia-a-leader-in-sustainable-business-and-corporate-responsibility/.

J2 Volkswagen (Social responsibility)
      (a) https://www.scientificamerican.com/article/the-science-behind-the-volkswagen-emissions-scandal/
      (b) https://www.volkswagen-group.com/en/diversity-and-inclusion-16087

J3 BP Oil (Social responsibility)
      (a) https://www.epa.gov/enforcement/deepwater-horizon-bp-gulf-mexico-oil-spill
      (b) https://www.george-business-review.com/corporate-social-responsibility-of-bp/
      (c) https://www.academia.edu/36199565/

J4 Wells Fargo (Social responsibility)
      (a) https://www.nbcnews.com/news/investigations/phony-bank-accounts-resurface-wells-fargo-twist-rcna98005
      (b) https://abcnews.go.com/Business/timeline-wells-fargo-accounts-scandal/story?id=42231128

K1 Microsoft Corporation (Diversity)
      (a) https://www.microsoft.com/en-us/diversity/default.aspx
      (b) https://blogs.microsoft.com/blog/2021/10/20/microsofts-2021-diversity-inclusion-report-demonstrating-progress-and-remaining-accountable-to-our-commitments/
      (c) https://blogs.microsoft.com/blog/2023/11/01/microsofts-2023-diversity-and-inclusion-report-a-decade-of-transparency-commitment-and-progress/

K2 Blick Shared Studios (Diversity)
      (a) https://blickstudios.org/blog/the-story-of-blick-shared-studios/
      (b) https://blickstudios.org/the-team/the-blick-story/
      (c) https://nervecentre.org/news/blog-reflecting-time-now-diversity-ni-creative-industries

L   Zappos (Fun)
      (a) https://thestrategystory.com/2021/04/13/zappos-customer-service-strategy/
      (b) https://aaronhall.com/insights/the-power-of-organizational-structure-how-zappos-strategy-drives-success/
      (c) https://www.bizjournals.com/bizjournals/how-to/growth-strategies/2014/01/zappos-customer-service.html

RESOURCES

1. *Scaling Up*, Verne Harnish.

2. *Business Adventures*, John Brooks.

3. *Built to Last: Successful Habits of Visionary Companies*, Jim Collins and Jerry I. Porras, 1994.

4. *Good to Great: Why Some Companies Make the Leap... and Others Don't,* Jim Collins, 2001.

5. *Start with Why: How Great Leaders Inspire Everyone to Take Action,* Simon Sinek.

6. *The Value of Core Values: Five Keys to Success through Values-Based Leadership,* Dr. Harry Kraemer.

7. *The Culture Code*, Daniel Coyle.

8. *The Value of Core Values*, Lisa Huetteman.

9. *Delivering Happiness,* Tony Hsieh.

10. *The Advantage*, Patrick Lencioni.

11. *Traction*, Gino Wickman.

12. The Life Planning Series (10 books), J. S. Wellman.

About the Author

The author graduated from the Business School at Indiana University and obtained a master's degree at Georgia State University in Atlanta. His first career was as a senior executive with a top insurance and financial institution, where he spent a number of years directing strategic planning for one of their major divisions.

In the 1990s he founded an online Internet business which he sold in 2010. He began to write and publish books and materials that led to an interest in personal life planning. This resulted in the Life Planning Series, the Life Planning Handbook, and books on Core Values.

The author, his wife, and two of his children and their families live in the Nashville, TN area.

WEBSITE: http://www.lifeplanningtools.com

AMAZON: www.amazon.com/author/jswellman

Contact Us

	www.lifeplanningtools.com info@lifeplanningtools.com	Website Email
Facebook	JSWellman	
	www.amazon.com/author/jswellman	**Author Page**
Life Planning Series	www.amazon.com/dp/B09TH9SYC4	
	www.lifeplanningtools.link/newsletter	**Monthly News Letter**

You can help

IDEAS and SUGGESTIONS: If you have a suggestion to improve this book, please let us know.

LEAVE A REVIEW: **https://www.amazon.com/dp/1952359511**

Thank you!

Create a high performing business culture and unleash your business potential.

www.ingramcontent.com/pod-product-compliance
Lightning Source LLC
Chambersburg PA
CBHW070929210326
41520CB00021B/6862